The Ultimate Guide to Opening Your Own Bubble Tea Shop

From Startup to Success

Christopher Cantrall

from various sources. Please consult a licensed professional before attempting any techniques outlined in this book.

By reading this document, the reader agrees that under no circumstances is the author responsible for any losses, direct or indirect, that are incurred as a result of the use of the information contained within this document, including, but not limited to, errors, omissions, or inaccuracies.

Table of Contents

Introduction

You may have always wanted to start your own business, but like most people, you haven't found that million-dollar idea yet. That is until you walked into a bubble tea shop. If the thought of opening a bubble tea shop has been more than just a fleeting thought in your head, then the good news is that there's no time like the present to do it. Bubble tea has never been more in demand than it is right now. Despite being a popular Asian drink, this colorful and delicious tea is taking the world by storm and its popularity just seems to keep rising. As a matter of fact, experts believe that the global bubble tea market is set to grow to and perhaps even exceed an astounding US$5.82 billion by 2032. Does this make you want to get in on this very lucrative action or what?

That said, starting your own bubble tea shop can be daunting—especially if you have never owned or perhaps even managed a business before. You may be even wondering if it's possible in a predominantly coffee-drinking society. Preliminary inquiries, though, would have undoubtedly highlighted one clear fact: There seems to be so much information to research, study, and consolidate, and that's before you've even drawn up the first draft of your business plan! How do you take your bubble tea dream from the planning stages to the corner shop in your town? The number one question potential bubble tea entrepreneurs always seem to be asking is—where does one even start?

Fortunately, my team and I have done the legwork for you. We've created easy-to-follow guides and practical solutions to make some of the general processes considerably easier. My love for the bubble tea industry started when I initially moved to Taiwan, where I have been living and working for the last six years. Working in one of the biggest bubble tea shops has given me valuable insight into the industry. So much so that my company, BubbleTeaology, provides premium bubble tea machines, custom cups, sealer films, and a variety of industry-specific training materials to bubble tea shops around the world. With this expert knowledge and hands-on approach, I know exactly what you need to get the process started. I'll share an extensive look at all aspects, from searching for the perfect location to creating your very first menu, and everything in between!

While opening your own bubble tea shop won't happen overnight or without its fair share of hiccups, I assure you that the journey will be a fun and interesting one. More importantly, it will not only be lucrative but a very rewarding process as well. Are you ready to start the learning process? Taking the first step is easier than you anticipated.

To get you started on your bubble tea journey, let's dive straight into the basics and take a look at its origins, market trends, and what makes this internet sensation such a hit (it helps to be sipping on your favorite bubble tea flavor as you read this!).

Chapter 1:

Basics of Bubble Tea

How did you first come to hear of bubble tea? My first experience with this awesome drink happened in Taiwan, where I've been working for several years. With its intriguing taste and an array of bright colors, it's easy to see why it's the talk of the town. However, before you even consider opening a bubble tea shop of any kind, it's important to understand the basics. In this chapter, I'll be giving you a rundown of how the wonderful world of bubble tea came about and why it's often referred to as "boba tea." What's in bubble tea? What are those little black balls that seem to be the secret ingredient? How is it served? And most importantly, what is the future of the bubble tea trend? Without further ado, let's dive right in and start answering these crucial questions.

Where Did Bubble Tea Originate?

If you're an absolute bubble tea noob, you might be forgiven for thinking that this delicious drink comes from China, like most other teas. However, the reality is that bubble tea was, in fact, invented in Taiwan in the 1980s at a small tea stand. In those days, tea stands would be set up outside schools, which enabled the children to buy a refreshing cup of tea after a long day of work and play. Considering that Taiwan, in those years, was not obsessed with soda drinks like the rest of the world, this wasn't uncommon at all to see a tea stand outside a school.

One of these tea stands seemed to be more popular than the others because its owner started adding a range of different fruit flavorings to her tea. Since this version of tea provided a sweeter, cooler taste than any traditional tea they were used to, the tea was an instant hit!

News of this fun, new tea spread, and the other concession owners started adding flavoring to their tea. For the most part, when flavoring is added to tea, it needs to be thoroughly shaken to create a well-mixed, all-around flavorful taste. Doing this formed bubbles in the drink, which is why the drink eventually became known as "bubble tea."

Who Is Liu Han-Chieh?

In 1983, the bubble tea concept was about to take on a whole new twist. Liu Han-Chieh, the founder of Chun Shui Tang Teahouse, encouraged his employees to come up with ideas for a new, creative mix. The teahouse manager, Lin Hsiu-Hui, had an appetite for *fenyuan*, or tapioca balls, and decided to add them to her milk tea, giving her something to chew as she sipped on her drink. While it seemed like a crazy idea, the new ingredient caught on, and this wondrous drink was added to Liu Han-Chieh's in-house menu. From that time, bubble tea with its black tapioca beads has been accredited to Liu-Han-Chieh.

Why the Term "Boba"?

Traditionally, tapioca pearls are made from starch and have a chewy texture. Ordinarily, these little spheres are black and are referred to as boba. To simplify, boba is just cassava root starch balls. The name you assign to your bubble tea depends largely on where you live. In Taiwan, bubble tea is often referred to as "pearl milk tea," "tapioca tea," or most popularly, boba. Chinese people refer to the tea as *zhēnzhū nǎichá*. In Los Angeles, bubble tea is really only known as boba, while for the folks on the East Coast, it's simply called bubble tea.

What Are the Basic Ingredients in Bubble Tea?

Whatever you decide to call your bubble tea, there's no denying that many variations have made their appearance over the years. However, in its most basic form, boba consists of black tea, milk, ice, and chewy tapioca pearls. Let's take a more extensive look at these specific ingredients:

- **Black tea:** Traditional boba is almost always made with black tea. More specifically, the common black tea blend is Assam tea. Although it's important to note that other black tea blends, such as Ceylon, can also be used, there might be subtle flavor differences. Other popular black tea brands to use include Earl Grey, Chai, and most breakfast teas.

- **Milk:** Many boba tea makers opt for whole dairy milk because it makes tea creamier. However, for dairy-free options, milk types such as cashew, almond, oat, soy, or Hokkaido milk are popular alternatives. Organic milk can also be used in some recipes.
- **Tapioca pearls:** As I've already mentioned, tapioca is simply cassava starch balls. Tapioca is generally available in grocery stores and health stores, and it can even be bought online. To enjoy the chewy consistency associated with bubble tea, tapioca pearls are a crucial ingredient. For the bubble tea noobs, boba pearls should always be chewed (not just swallowed) to unlock their delicious flavor.
- **Fruit extracts:** To provide a fruity flavor, boba makers often rely on flavored powder and syrup. Fresh and pureed fruit can also be added to enhance the fruity flavor and bright colors.
- **Sweeteners:** For additional sweeteners, simple sugar syrups, honey, or even fructose blends are added.
- **Coloring:** Artificial coloring is added to boba drinks to give them different, exciting colors. However, in many instances, the coloring is combined with the syrup.

- **Ice:** Boba makers will agree on one thing. No matter what type of tea, milk, or fruit flavoring you opt for, the secret to the perfect boba is its icy temperature. Crushed ice is the way to go. Although, of course, you can drink your boba warm if that's your preference.

With the extensive list of flavors and ingredients, the good news is that you'll easily find enough options to create a quality (and enticing) menu for your bubble tea business. Furthermore, hiring a creative boba barista will ensure that your menu is never short of interesting combinations.

How Is Bubble Tea Served?

Generally, all boba stores have similar outlays and menu styles. While available flavors may differ, the one thing that is consistent in all stores around the world is the way boba is served. For the most part, bubble tea is served in tall transparent cups, usually with the business logo featured prominently. A fat straw is provided because it allows you to sip up the tapioca balls so that they can be chewed as you drink the icy boba.

Why and How Did Bubble Tea Become an Overnight Global Sensation?

Boba's original rise to fame came in the 199os when it spread all over East and Southeast Asia. Areas such as Japan, Singapore, Mainland China, Vietnam, and Hong Kong saw bubble tea become increasingly popular with young people, who enjoyed the modern twist on an old favorite.

In Malaysia, like with so many other things in the modern world, boba saw its rise to fame stemming from social media. Bubble tea shops started creating differently flavored (and colored) boba and encouraged their customers to share images of their drinks on their social platforms. It wasn't long before these images started going viral, creating a social phenomenon that many young people wanted to be a part of.

The boba craze has expanded to just about every part of the globe, including the US. In fact, a recent survey from Towards Data Science (Chon, 2020) has listed the following interesting facts worth considering:

- A small city called Garden Grove with an estimated population of 170,000 people, is considered the boba capital of the US. According to the report, this quaint little town boasted about 33 bubble tea shops as of July 2020.

- The report also listed Charleston, South Carolina as the area with the most positive Yelp ratings, with an average rating of 4.63 across the town's five different bubble tea shops. However, since many businesses aren't necessarily listed on Yelp, this information might not be entirely accurate.
- If you're looking for the city with the most boba stores, then New York, with its 355 stores, actually has the highest number in the US.

Who Enjoys Boba?

If you love bubble tea nearly as much as I do, then your first response to that question might be, "Who doesn't?" You'll be delighted to know you're almost right. While boba is enjoyed by people of all ages, many different reports from around the world show that boba customers are often between the ages of 20–34. This makes it one of the top Gen Z and millennial drinks of choice. In fact, a recent consumer study done by Soocial.com shows that 94% of people between the ages of 20 and 29 have bought at least one cup of bubble tea within the last three months (Soocial, n.d.). The study also highlights that the drink is generally more popular with women than men. With the high customizability of this popular drink, it's easy for consumers to change their boba to suit their moods or personal preference.

What Is Bubble Tea's Future Potential and Upward Trend?

One of the top questions you might have researched extensively when the idea of a bubble tea shop started growing in your mind, was, undoubtedly: "What is the future potential upward trend?" After all, no one is going to invest in a business that seems to be catering to a short-term niche market. You don't want to own a niche business when everyone has moved on to the next fad, right? So, where does that leave the potential growth of the boba industry?

According to a report from Future Markets Insights, the current valuation of the bubble tea market is around US$2.50 billion in 2022. That said, the report also shows that the current market value is expected to reach a record high of US$5.82 billion by 2032. Essentially, this puts the bubble tea industry's projected growth rate at 8.8 percent between 2022–2032.

Furthermore, the boba industry can attribute its rapid expansion to the drink's diversity. Here are four key factors that will ensure that the market continues to see an upward trend:

- The continued rise in tea and nootropic drinks among the working-class populace of various societies.
- Ingredients are basic and can be customized to suit a wide variety of options, including low-

calorie and zero-fat options. Additionally, ingredients are easy to source all over the world, meaning there is very little need for importing resources.

- Rigorous in-house advertising on business social platforms ensures cost-reduced but highly effective advertising; these campaigns are literally being driven by customers, saving companies an extensive amount of money on traditional advertising.
- Franchise opportunities are on the rise, making it possible for more people to open more stores. A huge benefit here is the access to quality, verified products, which, in turn, creates customer buy-in because the brand is already established. Franchises offer opportunities with low startup costs, making this option increasingly appealing.

Key Takeaways

- Bubble tea originated in Taiwan, not China, as some people believe, and has been around since 1988.
- Tapioca balls create a unique consistency, adding to the drink's popularity.
- Basic bubble tea recipes are made up of black tea, milk, ice, and fruit extract.

- The average boba drinker is between the ages of 20–34 years old.
- The global trend of the boba industry is growing with no indication of slowing down, making it a lucrative business opportunity.

Chapter 2:

Deciding to Open a Boba

Shop

The thought of opening a bubble tea shop in the US might sound a little crazy at first. After all, it's no secret that the US is regarded as leaning more toward the coffee-drinking culture. In fact, Statistica.com shows the latest Starbucks outlets to be at 9,265 stores as of November 2022. That said, is there a place for a tea shop? More to the point, is there a market for a tea as exotic as boba?

Here's the good news. Studyfinds.org estimates that at least 63 percent of Americans enjoy a cup of tea every week (Melore, March 2022). Furthermore, 48 percent of respondents admitted to drinking tea daily. US stats also report that at least 95 percent of women and 81 percent of men have tried boba. That in itself should tell you that there is definitely a market for your boba shop! With that in mind, let's take a look at the key pointers to consider before you make the final decision to go ahead with your boba store dream.

How Does Bubble Tea Compare to Other Leading Non-Alcoholic Beverages?

When you're thinking about the market for bubble tea, it might be difficult to see it flourishing in areas where tea in general isn't the average drink of choice. However, market research has shown that trends are changing. Consumers are moving away from drinks that used to be consumed for the sake of quenching thirst. Instead, consumers are leaning toward healthier drinks with a wide range of flavor profiles. While it's true that boba has a higher sugar content than the average tea drink, the alternative is that bubble tea can be customized using less sugar and organic soy milk. Black tea can easily be substituted for a healthier green tea option. Unlike the average non-alcoholic beverage, boba's customizability makes it an incredibly popular choice.

What You Should Know Before Starting Up a Bubble Tea Business

If you're keen on setting up a boba shop, there's no doubt that you have been giving it a considerable amount of thought. In fact, you might already have been to a few stores to see what they're doing and to make a mental note of what seems to be going on behind the scenes. You may even have tried a bunch of different boba flavors to get an idea of what's potentially going on your menu and what's not. While that's a good place to start, there are a few other factors to consider before you invest too much time, effort, or even finances into starting your boba business. Let's review a few of the more common pointers to give some thought to:

Secure an Initial Investment

First things first. Before you start researching recipes, it's important to determine where you will get the finances to set up a successful boba shop. You'll need to factor in rental, signage, furniture, decor, machinery, supplies, advertising, general overhead, and employee salaries. Here, you will have a few options to consider:

- **Save up:** If you opt for the saving up option, it might take you longer than you initially anticipated to get your store going. It's important to establish exactly how much money you'll need so that you have a realistic goal to work toward. Factors such as machinery, supplies, property purchase or rental, advertising, signage, and, software systems are only a few of the necessities that you'll need to include in your initial budget. Alternatively, if you're going the franchise route, you need to check how much the various packages on offer will cost and which would suit your budget and your dream.

- **Request financing:** Many small business owners rely on loans specifically geared toward setting up small businesses. Speak to your bank or financial institution for more information about the processes and qualifying criteria. Be sure to check with them about tips for improving your credit record to make getting a small business loan considerably easier.
- **Approach investors:** Asking friends or family to invest in your business idea is another option to explore. Consider speaking to an attorney about the legal process to follow in this regard. That way, you'll be sure to have your money and business protected.

Acquire the Necessary Skills and Knowledge

Many potential business owners make the mistake of thinking that running a boba shop is easy because all you're doing is "making tea." It's important to keep in mind that your bubble tea shop is still a business, first and foremost. That means it should be run as such. To succeed, you will need plans and strategies in place to make the anticipated profits. Additionally, it's crucial to have a clear understanding of the bubble tea industry and how it works.

Key factors to understand include the following:

- how to make quality bubble tea
- what ingredients are required to make various types of bubble tea
- what types of machinery and equipment make the process easier and more professional
- how much revenue you need to make monthly to buy stock, maintain machinery, and pay overhead, and employees.
- the types of marketing ideas that make advertising your product more effective

When it comes to upskilling yourself in the bubble tea industry, be sure to do extensive research from a variety of different sources. That way, you will get a broad view of other business owners' experiences within the industry. Furthermore, get to know people already in the boba industry. Join social media groups and start networking with people who are already successful. The tips, tricks, and hacks you learn from these people are an easy way to learn the reality of the industry. I also recommend requesting ebooks or guidelines available for free on existing boba tea websites. A comprehensive example of this can easily be found on my website, BubbleTeaology.com.

Check Out the Local Competition

Another crucial factor to be aware of is the current bubble tea businesses in the area where you want to set up shop. While it might be your intention to outdo everyone else in your immediate vicinity with your innovative ideas, keep in mind that they have an existing customer base. Go to any boba stores in your area as if you are a customer. Order tea and speak to the staff as a customer—gauge their knowledge of the business and product in general.

This will give you an idea of their level of service, menu options, and customer service in general. Ultimately, this will let you know exactly what you're up against and it will highlight areas in which they may be lacking. You can then use this to your advantage. For instance, if they have a menu that's slightly lacking, then it already tells you that your menu should be jam-packed with options.

The Pros and Cons of a Boba Business

As with any other type of business, opening a bubble tea shop has its fair share of pros and cons. To assist you with making an objective, well-informed decision, I've compiled a list of the most significant pros and cons.

Pros

- **You're the boss:** There's something very rewarding about having to step out of a regular nine-to-five job and into your own business. Granted, it comes with its challenges, but the harder you work and the more you put into your business, the more rewarding it will be. Being your own boss puts you in charge of making decisions that will benefit your personal income.

- **Simple but effective business model:** A boba tea shop business model is relatively simple with products and necessary machinery easily accessible from suppliers that ship globally. This means that with the right effort, launching and growing your business is super easy. Moreover, the business model is tried and tested—whether it works depends on the effort you put in!

- **Processes are easy to learn**: Since boba is gaining popularity daily, more and more information is becoming available to assist potential business owners with all the information, guidelines, and tips needed to get their business off the ground. My company website—BubbleTeaology.com—provides excellent guides on all aspects of the developmental stages of your boba shop.

- **You're selling a popular product:** Let's face it. With the current boba trends, there is no better time to open a bubble tea shop. Additionally, since bubble tea is highly customizable, it's super easy to switch up your menu from time to time to prevent your selection from becoming boring.

- **Advertising isn't expensive:** One of the top concerns many new business owners have fixated on is the actual advertising of their businesses. How do you create brand awareness? And since advertising isn't cheap, this can be a concerning factor. However, boba is one of those products that advertises itself. All you have to do is have an engaging social media presence and encourage your customers to be active on it. That means you won't have to invest in major advertising costs to get your brand recognized (we will discuss more about social media advertising in a later chapter).

Cons

- **Start-up costs can be high:** Whether you regard the start-up costs as high or affordable largely comes down to the capital you have available. However, initially, you will have to purchase the correct machines and quality products (more on both of these aspects later). Never entertain the possibility of using "cheaper" products, as these are often of inferior quality, which will just cost you more in the long run. Additionally, having low-grade bubble tea-making machines will also affect the quality of your boba. Various franchise options may also have high initial costs.

- **Potentially low margins**: On average, the gross margins of your bubble tea business can be low. This is true especially in the beginning, as you learn your market and customer base. Most beginner boba shops work at an average margin varying between 20 to 30 percent, which often makes it a little challenging to acquire new products while trying to grow profits.

- **High taxes:** Since your boba shop falls into the small business category of things, you will be subject to self-employment taxes. The reality is that these taxes can often be unexpectedly high. To ensure that you aren't caught by surprise, always consider the tax requirements in the area and industry as part of your initial research.

- **Employee turnover may be high:** A common problem throughout the whole boba business is high employee turnover. While your dream may be to own a boba shop, not every employee's dream is to *work* in one. Many employees see working in a bubble tea shop as a stepping stone to the next opportunity. That means you will constantly be training new staff, which can be costly and time-consuming (more about hiring and training the right staff in a later chapter).

What Do You Need to Start a Bubble Tea Business?

While you're busy planning the ins and outs of your bubble tea shop dream, it helps to know what exactly you'll need to get your business on track. Here's a rundown:

1. **A storage space with a commercial kitchen:** The good news is that you can have a successful boba shop in a space of about 15 x 10 ft. So, you can get away with renting out a small space. The actual only major criterion here is the kitchen. You will need space to cook the tapioca. While you could do this on a countertop, this might put you in violation of specific health codes in your area. It's recommended to opt for a space with a kitchen (this also looks more professional to visitors).

2. **Create unique and tasty recipes:** While there are a bunch of basic recipes that most boba stores include on their menus, the key to success is to have several unique options. Here, you can consider a mix of the classics, some unique options, as well as what's trending in the

industry. With the wide variety of syrups on the market, it's easy to mix and match to find new flavorful combinations unique to your store. You will, however, need to practice making these combos well in advance. After all, you need to come across as a boba expert in your business! To ensure that your product doesn't go to waste, I recommend having a boba try-out party for your friends and family and getting their input about your flavor combinations as well as your tea brewing and tapioca cooking skills! As well, if you've already hired a boba barista at this point, be sure to include them in the menu creation process.

3. **An effective marketing strategy:** I can't stress this enough (you'll notice, I mention it a lot!). Your boba shop is a business and must be approached as such. What I mean by this is that "you may just be making tea," but your business needs to receive the same due diligence as a large organization would. That said, this includes a solid marketing strategy. Essentially, you need to consider how people will know where you are, what you're offering, and why you're better than the other boba stores in your area. If marketing isn't currently your strong point, I'll answer these questions in Chapter 6 to get you started.

4. **The right equipment:** The art of making boba might sound simple, but it still requires quality

machinery to ensure that you can produce a professional-looking product. This includes cups, the right types of straws, and the right clothing for your employees.

5. **Technology to run the business:** Many modern boba shops are resorting to using a point-of-sale (POS) system to take orders and track sales, inventory, and purchases. For this, you might be looking at one or two tablets and a Wi-Fi router. You will possibly also require an alarm system as part of your insurance criteria.

6. **Furniture:** Many bubble tea shops don't provide seating, and this actually isn't a requirement of the business model. However, many successful business owners recommend that if your space allows for it, you should include a few tables and chairs. If a customer stays in your store to enjoy their drink, then there's always the possibility of them ordering more drinks or other food products you might sell. Alternatively, if a customer buys a drink and leaves, your interaction with that customer is over in a few minutes.

7. **Staff:** Most importantly, you need quality staff. Where possible, opt for energetic people who either love the product as much as you do or have worked in the bubble tea industry long enough to bring valuable skills to your business (more about hiring the right employees in Chapter 7).

Estimated Costs of a Boba Shop

The first thought you had after the one that triggered the bubble tea business idea was most likely, "How much will a boba shop cost?" Generally, there isn't a specific one-size-fits-all answer here. Factors such as the size of your store, products on offer, rental, employee costs, and overhead costs vary between different places. With that in mind, a boba business can cost anywhere between $75,000 and $200,000.

For the most part, the cost of your real estate will be the most expensive factor to contend with. Will you be renting or buying? If you're buying a property, you might have a loan or mortgage to consider. It's worth mentioning that the average cost of real estate in the US runs in the region of $18 per square foot. Of course, this is also subject to location. Prime property inside malls or student buildings might be more expensive.

Typical Expenses for the Average Boba Shop

As I've already mentioned, each bubble tea shop is unique and will have its own specific costs. There are, however, a few standard expenses that are common to all boba shops. The most common are listed below:

- utilities (rental, energy bill, insurance)
- POS systems
- employee salaries
- initial costs for signage decor

- bubble tea machines (tea makers, ice makers)
- kitchen equipment to cook necessary ingredients
- disposable serving products (cups, straws, napkins)
- various ingredients (tea, tapioca, sugar, toppings, syrups)
- marketing costs (logo design and placing on disposable products)

Estimated Profits From Boba Shops

Again, there is no one-size-fits-all answer. However, here's a simple formula that will help you determine the average revenue you can expect to make annually:

Average selling price per cup x average amount of cups sold per day x 350 days

Once you have your estimated annual revenue, simply deduct your yearly expenses from this amount to establish what your profit will be. To simplify this calculation even further, I'm going to use a working example from my website as an example:

Let's start by looking at how much it costs to make a single cup of boba. Keep in mind that this is calculated per cup.

Item Needed Per Cup	Item Cost Per Cup
Tea	$0,05
Flavoring	$0,42
Liquid fructose	$0,05
Tapioca pearls	$0,20
Custom logo cup	$0,06
Cup seal	$0,01
Straw	$0,01
Total cost per cup	**$0,80**

On average, a boba shop can sell x100 cups of bubble tea per day. In fact, some established stores can easily sell considerably more. With that in mind, it also helps to know your break-even point; that means the point you need to reach to not be running at a loss. If your expenses are $75,000 per year, any revenue total below that means you are running at a loss. In short, you should never spend more than you earn!

Reasons Boba Shops Fail

No one wants to entertain the thought of their dream business failing, especially when it seems as though boba is possibly one of the easier industry types to start in. My intention in discussing reasons why boba shops fail is by no means an attempt to put a damper on your dream. However, it's always been my belief that understanding why stores fail gives potential business owners a better grasp on the mistakes to avoid from the get-go.

I've heard many customers say, "It's just tea. How hard can it be to make and sell tea?" My answer has always been: "There's a difference between making bubble tea and making *exceptional* bubble tea." Let's take a look at a few of the more common reasons boba shops fail:

1. **Inferior tasting boba:** Many customer review platforms cite poor-tasting products as the number one reason why customers don't return to a particular bubble tea shop. Don't assume because you're "just making tea" and following a particular recipe that you're assured of a great-tasting product. Test your recipes beforehand and tweak them where necessary. Be sure to do a taste and quality test on all new boba drinks your barista recommends adding to the menu. Quality control should be a top priority. In Chapter 10, I'll share some tried and tested bubble tea recipes that you can easily use to get your menu started.

2. **Poorly prepared tapioca pearls:** In many instances, the reason for a poor-tasting boba stems from incorrectly prepared tapioca pearls. Since the tapioca pearls are what make boba special and unique, this is one element that should be right at all times. If you're not entirely sure how to prepare tapioca, it's vital to not only learn but perfect this skill before you open your doors. If you're hiring a barista, test their tapioca-making skills before hiring them. In Chapter 10, I'll share the process of preparing your tapioca pearls.

3. **Failure to have a robust business plan:** Opening something as "simple" as a tea shop might leave some new business owners under the impression that a business plan isn't really necessary. After all, is it really that difficult? It's important to realize that business plans aren't just for securing finances, or for larger organizations. Every business should have a plan to guide the flow of the business. Furthermore, a quality plan will highlight business goals, budgeting, startup costs, and profit distribution. Be sure to check out Chapter 4 for everything you need to know about creating the perfect business plan.

4. **Purchasing poor quality products:** The initial capital required to set up a bubble tea shop might leave some business owners opting for lower quality machines and products in a

wayward effort to potentially reduce costs and increase margins. Since boba tea is so popular, it's almost a guarantee that your customers would have tasted great boba somewhere else and will instantly know if your product is inferior. Ingredients should always be fresh and prepared correctly. In Chapter 5, I'll be sharing some top-notch products that every boba shop shouldn't be without!

5. **Lack of effective marketing**: Despite living in a digital world where you don't need to spend a lot of money on advertising, many boba businesses still don't have an effective marketing plan in place. Be sure to create an engaging social presence. Additionally, you can offer free samplings and community contests to create initial awareness of your brand. I'll explore marketing in considerably more detail in Chapter 6.

6. **Badly managed business:** Whether you're trying to sell boba or sneakers, the reality is that a badly managed business will very seldom succeed. Don't assume that your employees have your business's best interests at heart, especially if you're not hands-on or on the premises often. A successful boba shop cannot be bought and left for employees to run. In Chapter 7, I'll provide you with some tips for hiring effective employees.

7. **Badly chosen location:** You can have the best machines, superior ingredients, and outstanding marketing, however, all that will mean very little if your store is located in the wrong spot. How do you go from choosing the cheapest rental spot to finding the best location? What factors determine a good location? In Chapter 3, I'll explain how to go about doing market surveys and also share a few tips to help you choose the best location.

8. **Failure to keep up with current market trends:** It should go without saying that bubble tea has significantly evolved in the years since it was first created. Additionally, many of your competitors will be eager to experiment with new products and flavor combinations. Your client base will expect to see new and innovative drinks and products on your menu or they'll go elsewhere. Always offer a menu that features a combination of classics, new options, and even designer variations. Having a variety of ingredients on hand will make it easy to offer your customers the opportunity to customize their drinks according to their personal choice. In Chapter 8, I'll share a few pointers about how to create a unique but engaging menu.

Key Takeaways

- Boba is currently one of the more popular non-alcoholic drinks.
- You will need a considerable initial investment to cover the start-up costs, which could range anywhere between $75,000 and $200,000.
- Necessary knowledge and bubble making skills are essential to compete with other boba stores in the same area.
- It's crucial to compare all the pros and cons to assist you with making an informed decision.
- Review the typical store-related expenses and determine how they fit into your budget.
- Calculate a break-even point and ensure that you never spend more than you're earning.
- Use the list of reasons why boba shops fail as a guideline to avoid similar scenarios in your own business.
- A well-planned and properly executed structure will lead to considerable profits and a sustainable business.

Chapter 3:

Location, Location, and

Location

There's an old cliched expression in real estate that everyone's heard many times: "Location, location, location." There's a reason this overused phrase still rings true. Without the right location, you may as well be selling bubble tea from home! Once you've confirmed that you're definitely going to go ahead and create your dream boba shop, the next crucial step to consider is the location of your store. Whether you're already in an existing business, or you're starting a company for the first time, you've no doubt heard of the importance of location. For instance, if the target market in your area is primarily students, would it make sense to set up a shop in the industrial part of town? Obviously not.

With that in mind, how do you go about looking for the best location for your boba shop? It's important to note that finding the perfect location is about a lot more than finding cheap rental options in your area! So, if you're doing this for the first time, where do you start? This chapter takes a look at the following crucial factors that will help you identify the perfect location:

- market surveys
- site surveys
- tips for choosing the best location in your area
- store layouts
- lease negotiation
- health department regulations

How to Do a Market Survey on and Offline

Just because a place doesn't already have an existing boba shop doesn't mean it must have one. It could be that other potential business owners did feasibility studies and found the area not conducive to their specific target market. With that said, it's always an excellent idea to do your own market surveys in the area. Doing this will tell you exactly what type of people live and work in the region and if boba tea is something they'd be interested in. How are market surveys done?

Essentially, market surveys can be done on and offline. If you have the means, it's well worth the effort to do both types. This way, you will be assured that you're not investing time, money, and effort on a gut feeling alone. Let's take a look at the difference between doing on and offline surveys.

Online Surveys

Essentially, there are four general types of online surveys—employee engagement, customer satisfaction, market research, and customer feedback. You'll be choosing the market research option for this first type of survey. For starters, you'll need to register with an online survey platform. One of the more popular options is SurveyMonkey, but you can go with anyone that you prefer. Once on the platform, you set up your survey and draw up the questions that will help you identify a potential target market. Some popular questions to ask include the following:

- Are you interested in buying bubble tea?

- Which current flavor is your favorite? (Here, you can list 3–5 of the top trending options and you can include one or two designer options)

- Do you prefer a buy-and-go service or a sit-down and enjoy?

- Which of these factors helps you choose the best bubble tea? (Price, quality, quantity, brand, flavor types)

- Do you find the proposed price range reasonable? (Here, you would list your proposed price list as "Large cup - $2,50, Medium cup - $2,00, Small cup - $1,50, Baby cup - $1,00. Of course, your prices may vary, depending on your own specific costs.)

- What age group are you in? (15–25, 26–35, 36–45, older)

Keep in mind that these questions are just a guideline and you can amend them to suit your unique survey. You can also add questions about your area, but don't ask too many technical questions about branding as that may not interest the respondent. However, don't ask too many questions in general, as your audience might get bored and exit the survey altogether.

Offline Surveys

Generally, offline surveys are done using an application tool that you use to collect data from users and potential customers without needing an active internet connection. These types of surveys work well if you're walking around town or you're in the mall chatting to people about how they regard a boba shop potentially opening in the area. You can also promote this type of survey on your social media platforms as well as various chat groups. However, specify that the survey should only be taken by people who are in the area you're planning to launch your boba business. Once again, SurveyMonkey and Google Forms are just two options to consider. These types of apps can be assessed by both iOs and Android users.

How to Do Site Surveys and How to Select the Flagship Location

As the term dictates, a site survey refers to the examination of a potential location to determine if it meets the required criteria for your boba business. Unlike a market survey, you can't do a site survey online. Rather, you need to visit the site and the surrounding area to determine if the location is conducive to your intended bubble tea business. Think of it as being similar to the way you view a home before deciding to rent it. When doing a site survey, ensure that you can adequately answer the following questions:

1. Is the area exposed to your intended target market? (Do they walk or drive past there often enough to see your shop?)
2. Does the area have sufficient parking? (Will your target market be able to easily reach your store?)
3. What businesses are located around the premises? How will this affect the customer experience? (For instance, a shop next to a noisy factory won't be as inviting as a quaint little corner shop.)
4. Does the proposed cost or rental validate what you'll be getting in return?
5. Is the building in decent condition, or will there be significant remodeling done? At whose cost

will this be done? How long will this take and how will it affect your proposed opening date?

6. Is there a place for signage? (This includes on the building and even storefront or sidewalk.)

7. Does the storefront look out onto passing traffic?

8. Does the space have a commercial kitchen and sufficient counter space for the necessary machines? Will you be able to fit a few tables and chairs into the space?

9. Are there any particular zoning restrictions to that specific area? (Although, in most instances, there shouldn't be any for a space as simple as the one required to facilitate a boba shop, but be sure to check anyway!)

10. Is the store secure or will you need to install a security system?

Tips for Choosing the Best Bubble Tea Shop Location

If you've never owned, managed, or worked at a store before, you might find choosing the right location a bit challenging. I've compiled a few tips to highlight what you should be looking for when you start shortlisting potential options.

1. Consider the Amount of Passing Traffic

The most essential aspect of any boba shop's success has to do with the amount of passing traffic that your store will get. While it's true that a great bubble tea shop will eventually build up a large number of boba enthusiasts who become loyal customers, you will still need new business. Passing traffic is the best way to create awareness and generate new business. A few top areas that generate the best passing traffic are:

- in busy malls or shopping centers (where there aren't already specialty tea or coffee shops)
- close to or in office parks and centers
- busy high streets that see a lot of walking and driving traffic
- around universities, colleges, or areas with a considerable amount of local and even international students
- areas that are on the way to or from public transport, such as close to a bus stop or train station (this is one of the better options because you are guaranteed a steady stream of traffic most days of the week)
- traffic should be consistent, which means that your store should be relatively busy most days of the week to ensure that you'll generate

expected turnover (being busy two days a month when there's an event at a nearby location won't work well for your boba business)

2. *Available Space for Signage*

No matter how great the space is inside your boba shop, you should also have sufficient branding on the outside. Without the correct signage, passing traffic won't be curious about what you're selling. Therefore, you'll want a commercial property with enough space to put up eye-catching signage that not only draws attention but also indicates what's being sold inside. Many successful boba stores make use of signage both on the building and around the storefront. Keep in mind that not all passers-by will look up to read your signs, so it's a good idea to have some form of signage on the sidewalk they walk past.

Be sure to check the local regulations regarding the types of signage allowed on and around the storefront. Generally, most successful bubble tea shops use these guidelines to ensure effective signage:

- Signs must stand out and be as bright and eye-catching as your boba drinks.

- Brand name and business logo must be displayed clearly and should be legible from across the street.
- Signage should always be visible in the street so that it's easy for referrals to find.

3. Consider the Neighbors

The type of neighbors you have will play a large role in how successful you will be. For instance, opening your shop next to a Starbucks might not be the best idea. However, opening your shop next to a busy nail or hair salon will provide you with access to their customer base who may want a boba while they wait for their appointment. Ideally, you want to be close to businesses that cater to the same demographic or target market that you do. Since you can add a variety of healthy boba options to your menu, setting up your store near a gym or exercise center is also worth considering.

4. Review All the Zoning and Area-Related Issues

There's no such thing as the "perfect location." Some are just better than others, but all have their own issues to contend with. Here, you want to check how the policies of the area affect your business. For instance, are there zoning laws that regulate your type of signage? If the space is in a shopping mall, will your trading hours be determined by yourself or by mall regulations? How easy will it be for your suppliers to access the back of your store when dropping off stock? Or will they be able to drop it off in front without inconveniencing customers?

Boba Store Layout–What to Look For

Part of finding the perfect location involves knowing what type of layout you should create for your boba store. Generally speaking, the layout you design depends on your budget and the available space. Keep in mind, though, that bigger spaces often require higher rentals and overhead expenses. It might be a good idea to start with a small to medium-sized space if you're working with a limited budget.

Since a boba shop is all about the simplicity of great-tasting bubble tea, you don't need the whole restaurant experience. That said, your space needs to have a commercial kitchen and the right equipment. Ideally, the proposed premises should have the following:

- front ordering area (where boba is ordered over a counter and where the point-of-sale system is)
- back kitchen (where the tapioca and other ingredients can be prepared and stored according to local health regulations)
- small interior seating space for customers who wish to sit down and enjoy their tea rather than take it with them; for some, it might be an escape from the office!

When you're considering the size of the kitchen you're going to need, this list of equipment needed for a well-functioning bubble tea kitchen might help. You'll need:

- **Stove**: electric or gas, depending on the available outlets in your store
- **Tea brewer:** to brew your black or green tea "just right"
- **Fructose dispenser:** allows you to create consistency for all your boba drinks
- **Shaker machine:** creates the right consistency for your boba by correctly mixing various powders and syrups
- **Sealer machine:** ensures that your cups are sealed correctly and professionally
- **Fridge:** one large enough for a considerable amount of stock
- **Ice maker:** along with storage

- **Storage cupboards for stock and cups:** for health reasons, the stock shouldn't be stored directly on the floor, even if it's in plastic buckets
- **Multiple sinks:** this is to ensure that your employees can easily clean up spills, and wash the kitchen counters, machinery, tables, and of course their hands! This will also ensure that your shop adheres to any post-pandemic regulations that might be in place in your area.
- Be sure to check for the right types of electric sockets and outlets to ensure that your business doesn't suffer constant power outages or malfunctioning equipment.
- Depending on the area where you live, it may be necessary to change the types of power outlets you have available, as this will affect the way some machines work.

Additional pointers to keep in mind when you're designing and calculating the space required for your kitchen have to do with the general flow in your workspace. Ideally, you don't want employees in each other's way, and you also don't want to create a crowded space. This does not look unprofessional but makes the customers feel like they need to get out there as quickly as possible. As I mentioned, a quick in-and-out exchange with a customer only results in a few minutes of interaction and only a small sale. So, to improve the flow in your boba shop, consider these pointers:

- **Create a specific cooking section:** Place the cooking equipment together in one area, away from the ordering area.
- **Separate the tea creations area:** Tea creation should happen in a separate section of the kitchen—this is where the toppings are added and the boba is assembled.
- **Final steps:** Many boba (and even coffee) shops keep the machinery needed for the final steps near the point-of-sale—this is to provide the customer with the freshest and best-looking brew. Customers also enjoy seeing their drinks being finished. In a boba setting, this is usually just the shaker and sealer. However, these machines mustn't be in the way of tending to customers as they pay.

Negotiating a Lease

When you've identified the best possible site for your store, it's time to discuss and negotiate a lease with the property owner or landlord. This can be a daunting process if you've never discussed property rentals. And let's face it, landlords can be quite intimidating! That's why I've included a few common tips to help you negotiate the best possible lease agreement for your new business.

1. **Prepare**

By the time you meet the landlord, you should already have determined your rental budget. Additionally, you should have a list of absolute must-haves as well as a list of nice-to-haves. Must haves include the kitchen space, electric outlets, and possibly even parking. Nice-to-haves would be factors that will add to your business but not necessarily determine its success. Outside seating could be an example of this. Depending on the particular space, parking may be nice if the premises are already accessible by foot traffic.

2. **Consider Using an Agent or Property Lawyer**

If you aren't too confident in your lease negotiating skills and if your budget allows, I recommend getting a property lawyer involved in the process. Not only are property lawyers well-versed in the laws surrounding commercial leases, but they also know a few tricks to get you the best deal possible.

3. **Look at Several Locations**

There's no denying it. When you see a particular spot, you'll know if it's the right one. However, that said, it's important to have options. Setting your sights on only one location could set you back if the negotiations with the landlord failed. Use the same site survey criteria to assess a few potential options. This will give you other choices to consider if you have to walk away from an unreasonable negotiating process. Don't put yourself in an "I don't have a choice" situation.

4. Verify the Measurements

It's not unusual for each commercial tenant to change a particular space to suit their needs. For instance, they could add drywall, shelves, or counters which in some instances aren't removed before the new tenant views the space. That said, you're potentially renting the *usable* space, and if previous alterations have been done, the available square footage you need might not be what's been listed on the original building specs. Since rent is based on square footage, it's crucial to check this yourself to ensure you're not left shortchanged at the end of the day. In situations where the measurements are smaller than the landlord is claiming, you might be able to negotiate a discount on your potential lease amount.

5. Negotiate the Fixturization Process

It's very unlikely that you are going to move into the space as it is. You will need to renovate the space to fit your boba store requirements. This includes painting, setting up the kitchen, attending to the signage and seating area, and in some cases adding the front counter spaces. It can be quite draining to be expected to pay rent in the month or two that it takes to remodel and set up your bubble tea shop. After all, you aren't generating revenue during this period, yet your rent will still be due. Your property lawyer will advise you to request one of two solutions here:

- **Landlord prepares the space:** In this instance, the landlord will opt to renovate the space to your basic requirements. This means that their contractors will remove the previous tenant's alterations, paint, and ensure that counters and electrical outlets are added. They will then hand you what is commonly referred to as a "clean building," where you just add your signage and in-store decor.

- **You do the renovations yourself:** In instances where you will do the renovations yourself, a landlord might offer you free rent for the period it takes you to set up your boba shop. In many instances, this won't exceed 120 days if there are specialized permits that need to be requested. Although, with the basic setup for a boba shop, it's unlikely that you will need special permits. This is referred to as the "fixturization period." To streamline the process, opt for a space that requires very little fixing-up.

6. Discuss Potential Free Rent Promotions

This is one of those instances where your property lawyer's bag of tricks will come in handy. Many landlords have a way to compromise on your request to pay lower rent. They will instead offer you a "rent-free promotion," which means there will be periods during the lease that you qualify for free rent. For instance, the landlord may offer you one free month for every 12 months, which can save you an average of 8.3 percent over a three-year lease cycle. By offering you this promotion, a landlord doesn't have to lower their base rent and won't risk affecting future negotiations. This is also a great opportunity to include regular utilities that would be due in the free month.

7. Insist on a "No Competitor" Clause

If your potential space is in a building with several other stores, it's essential to insist on a clause that prevents them from renting other spaces to other boba shop owners. You may even go so far as to insist that the clause over any type of tea or coffee shop, since any one of these can sell boba tea products. This would put them in direct competition with you and would jeopardize your ability to generate sufficient revenue.

8. Include a "Force Majeure" Clause

Depending on where your store is located, a force majeure clause can be a crucial part of the negotiation process. Essentially, this refers to situations that might legally excuse your lease responsibilities. I'm, of course, referring to unforeseen events such as war, labor strikes, and weather phenomena like hurricanes and tornadoes. These would be commonly referred to as acts of God and are the same as the clauses on most insurance policies. Having this clause in effect will ensure that you don't run into a financial mess when any of these instances prevent you from paying your rental obligations.

Health Department Regulations to Consider

Before signing any lease or rental documents, it's crucial to review the health department regulations for your specific area. This is especially important since you'll be serving customers something they can consume. Product storage and preparation areas need to meet certain criteria and there may be certain licenses and permits that need to be obtained before you're allowed to open for business. Your first order of business should always be to review these criteria, as this can result in a fine or business closure if your boba shop is found to be non-compliant. As part of certain safety requirements, some areas may require special certifications such as UL or NSF for machines to be used in your boba shop. Be sure to purchase appropriately certified equipment if this is the case in your area. The UL or NSF specifications are not criteria required to make the machines work, but rather form part of the safety requirements within different areas—I will discuss this in more detail in Chapter 5, when I share a few of the top machines to consider.

Boba Shop on a Budget

It has to be said that your boba shop doesn't have to be in an actual store if your budget isn't as great as you'd like. After all, the original bubble tea idea originated from a concession stand. The crucial element to keep in mind here is a sufficient way to cook tapioca. If you've got that sorted, any of the following options could work equally well:

- food stand
- small kiosks at a craft market or student lodgings
- food truck

Key Takeaways

- Doing extensive market surveys will help you identify where your target market is.
- Site surveys are necessary to identify and to shortlist potential prime locations.
- Always consider factors such as foot traffic, signage, branding opportunities, and zoning regulations before deciding on a spot.
- Review the local health department regulations for all the spots on your shortlist.
- Consider the crucial factors of a store layout for your potential store—a commercial kitchen with sufficient food storage facilities is a must.
- Negotiating a lease requires some practice, and if possible, opt for a property lawyer wherever possible—this way you'll get access to a host of different tips and tricks to negotiate the best possible lease.

- For potential business owners with a limited budget, streamlined options such as food trucks and concession stands are an innovative way to start.

Chapter 4:

Create a Business Plan

We've all heard the expression, "Plan the work, work the plan." That said, having a business plan in place for your bubble tea store is a clear way to organize all your business processes. Furthermore, it shows potential investors or financial institutions that you have evaluated potential running costs, devised marketing strategies, and created a workable plan to deal with any risks. No matter how easy you may think running a boba business is, every new business venture needs a business plan.

For many potential boba shop owners, this step can be the most frustrating. In my dealings with various clients, I hear one question more than any other— "where does one even start when setting up a bubble tea business?" My answer to these people is always the same: Start with the business plan. Create a plan of what you want to do, and perfect all the aspects of your plan.

The Top Benefits of Having a Robust Business Plan

Understanding how a business plan will benefit your boba shop will highlight the importance of why you need one. Consider these pointers when you're drawing up your plan:

1. **Creates an overview of the whole business:** Effective business planning creates an accurate overview of your organization.

2. **Identifies and prioritizes goals:** Setting up a business is a lot of hard work and can be very time-consuming. It's also very difficult to do everything by yourself. A business plan helps you keep track of what needs to be done as well as during which stages of your planning. It's an excellent resource to help you allocate your resources, time, and effort more strategically.

3. **Creates milestones:** If you want to make a success of your boba business, you can't start it with a "let's see what happens" attitude. Effective business planning assists you in creating milestones you and your team can work toward. Once you define these goals and then write them down, print them out, or create them digitally, they become visible goals.

4. **Assists with obtaining finances:** Are you going to require lender or investor assistance to

obtain the capital required to make your boba dream come true? If that's the case, an investor or lending facility isn't simply going to take your word for it that your business will be profitable. They want to see that you have analyzed every aspect of the business and its potential profit margins. These potential lenders or investors want to know that there is a plan in place for them to either get their money back or see a positive return on their investment. A detailed business plan with well-researched strategies and concise financial and marketing plans is the best way to portray your confidence in your and your team's ability to make the plan work.

5. **Facilitates course adjustment:** There's no denying that things don't always go according to plan. For instance, you might have anticipated a five percent growth in your business in the first year, but in reality, you only showed a three percent growth with a somewhat lower gross margin than you had anticipated. Does that mean your plan is no longer valid? Of course not! What it means is you need to highlight an area of your goal that needs to be readjusted in order to get you back on track to your five-year plan. By tweaking your plan at your monthly, quarterly, bi-annual, and annual reviews, you will be sure that your business recovers the shortfall.

Creating a Business Plan–Where to Start

If you're not sure how to start creating your business plan, the good news is that my team can easily help you with that. My website—again, bubbleteaology.com—offers a fully developed business plan that covers the most crucial points to consider. I've also listed the general order in which these pointers should be structured, with a brief description of what they're about.

1. Executive Summary

An executive summary states the purpose of your boba business. Essentially, you'll include the entire cost involved and when you'd like to launch the business. Sub pointers to consider as part of the executive summary are:

- **Products and operations:** Here, you'll specify that your primary revenues will come from the sale of various bubble tea products. Some plans highlight that their products will be made from fresh ingredients which can include fresh fruit. In terms of operations, it's important to highlight that orders are counter-service based. You will also need to specify that marketing will be done via the business's extensive online presence. Keep in mind that you will need to create a website and pages on various social platforms.

- **Financing:** This part covers the exact amount of financing required. This is especially relevant if your business plan forms part of a loan or financing request. Be specific about what the funds will be used for. The three general aspects here are the acquisition or rental of property, capital required for equipment, and the working capital needed for the early expenses of the business. Be ready to give your potential investors or financiers an exact breakdown of the costs and quantities of products required. Many potential business owners substantiate this section with quotes or estimates from vendors.

- **Future business opportunities**: It's important to not seem overeager in this section. While your goal may be to own a chain of boba shops, potential investors may be hesitant to invest if you come across as too eager. After all, you need to establish your first shop as well as your brand. In most cases, potential business owners will specify that no future developments can occur until the current business is established and current loans paid off. This is usually listed as being between three and five years.

- **Revenue forecasts:** In this section, you list the estimated growth pattern for the first five years. You will have to do extensive calculations here based on the cost of the product, expected sales, overhead expenses, and eventual profit.

2. Financing

This section is based on an extensive breakdown of the financing required for your boba shop. Essentially, it's a more detailed explanation and breakdown of the money you're asking for.

- **Funds required:** List the basic startup costs that the funds will be used for. This generally includes location purchase and/or rental, development costs, working capital, initial marketing, fees, and license requirements as well as product costs. In this section, you'll mention any costs that will be contributed by you or any other investors.
- **Investor equity:** Do you require additional outside investor equity? Many boba entrepreneurs don't require outside investor involvement if they can get funding from their financial institution.

- **Management equity:** Will the owner retain 100 percent ownership in the business, or will ownership be shared? If so, how will the shares be divided and who are the other parties? Will it be a partnership?
- **Board of directors:** Will the business have a board of directors? Usually, boba entrepreneurs serve as the directors of their own businesses.
- **Potential exit strategy:** In the event of the business failing, what exit strategy do you have in place to recover the bulk of the outstanding costs? For the most part, this covers pointers such as selling the company to a larger organization if it becomes necessary. If this were to happen, what do you value your company and assets at?

3. Operations

In this section of the business plan, the day-to-day operations are discussed in more detail. For instance, will your store only sell boba teas? What type of ingredients will be required? If you're going to source your products locally, be sure to mention this, as this contributes to your local economy. It will also emphasize that you aim to minimize costs wherever possible. Additionally, discuss the cost per beverage and the estimated gross margin per sale. For many boba shop startups, this amount centers around $6,00 per item at a potential gross margin of 84%. This is based on the affordable cost of products and ingredients.

If your business is going to be focusing on sustainability in its business practices, be sure to mention how you'll be doing that in this section. Since bubble teas have several health benefits, it's a good idea to emphasize that in this section as well. Furthermore, how will the store's design and layout resonate with the qualities of the brand and product? For instance, you can mention that your boba shop will strive to create a modern aesthetic with minimalistic decor made from recycled materials. If the premises that you're considering need to have any alterations done, it's important to mention this and specify whether or not the property landlord is involved in this process or if you're carrying the cost.

4. Overview of the Organization

The overview of your organization refers to the general information about your company.

- **Registered name**: List the proposed name of your business as well as the state, the date the company was registered, and the type of company your business has been listed as. For the most part, it should be an LLC—a limited liability company.
- **Commencement of operations:** This refers to the anticipated date you're expecting to open

your store. It might not be possible to establish the exact date if you're waiting for funding, so you can just provide the estimate such as "first to the second quarter of 2023."

- **Mission statement:** Every business should have a mission statement. This is the primary goal of your business in the simplest terms. An example could be: "Our company strives to provide (area name) consumers with a broad selection of high-quality bubble tea and related products at an affordable price."

- **Vision statement:** A vision statement differs from a mission statement in that it's more specific to the business goals. Essentially, you want to mention that your boba business aims to generate X amount of revenue within the first three or five years of business.

- **Organizational objectives:** Generally, organizational objectives highlight the simple day-to-day plans that will help your business grow. List pointers such as developing strong, working relationships with local vendors, abiding by local health regulations within the food and beverage industry as well as using local media influencers to increase brand awareness.

- **Organizational values:** What ethics will your boba business abide by to ensure transparency? Some examples of this include providing a stable work environment for employees, complete and transparent disclosure of all financial transactions, and continually providing a stream of income within the legal parameters of the bubble tea-making and selling industry.

5. Strategic Analysis

In the strategic analysis section, you discuss different factors within the bubble tea environment in your area, as well as in the industry in general. You'll also highlight how this will impact your boba shop and what—if anything—you're going to do about it.

- **External environmental analysis:** How many competitors are there in your local area; will you be the first boba shop in your town or city? Also mention that boba shops are a rapidly growing industry and list a few of the reasons they're so popular. Additionally, highlight how this industry is taking off in the US (or whatever country you're in). Furthermore, it's always beneficial to your business plan to add as many authoritative statistics as possible. I'll cover this in more detail in a later chapter.

- **Industry analysis:** How does the boba shop business model fit into the restaurants and eateries industry in the US (or, again, in the country you're in)? For instance, very few people know that quick service and counter-service food businesses—such as boba shops—generate an average of $300 billion per annum in revenues.

- **Customer profile:** What is the demographic your boba shop is targeting? For instance, how old are they? How much do you anticipate them spending with each visit? Generally, this is calculated at $6 to $12 per visit, which is about two cups of boba. How far from the location will your target market be? The average estimate here is five miles from your boba shop. If your store will be near a location where your target market spends a lot of time, or features as passing traffic, mention it here as well. For instance, if your target market is generally between 18 and 30, them being near a school or college is beneficial to you.

- **Competitive analysis:** In this section, you'll list the bubble tea businesses in your area. Specify how you will compete with them—what will your boba shop do differently? If your store has e-commerce-based ordering functionality (where customers order online and go to the store to collect), this is the ideal place to mention it. In short, what will you do to ensure that your boba store is economically stable?

6. Key Strategic Issues

Setting up your boba business is one thing. Keeping it sustainable and generating a lucrative profit requires constant tweaking. This section refers to how you're going to ensure that your business remains profitable.

- **Sustainable competitive advantage:** What are the reasons your boba business will remain successful? One reason could be that your bubble tea products will never be priced lower than 500 percent markup over direct acquisition cost. The visibility of your store and an effective ordering system also factors in this part of your business plan.
- **The basis for growth:** How will your bubble tea store grow? Extensive and vigorous marketing both online and in the surrounding location are strong points to elaborate on here. In short, what will facilitate growth in the area?

7. Marketing Plan

Every business needs a robust marketing strategy in place. In this section, you'll highlight the key factors of the types of marketing plans you have in place to make your brand and your product known in your area.

- **Marketing objectives:** Two prominent points worth mentioning here are that your boba shop will establish and maintain strong connections with local and/or regional vendors and suppliers. You should also mention your company website and social media platforms and how you'll use these to market your brand and product, as well as to engage with existing and potential customers. This is important because a lot of the bubble tea culture features online marketing where customers share product images and general brand experiences.

- **Revenue forecasts:** In short, how much revenue and profit do you anticipate? Create a forecast for the first five years. Creating a five-year plan shows potential investors or lenders that you are both professional and serious about your business.

- **Revenue assumptions:** If you've calculated your revenue forecasts in a table format, then your revenue assumptions will be an overview and explanation of what you based those calculations on. Break it down by year to create a professional structure. Be sure to highlight yearly revenue and gross profit.

- **Marketing strategies:** It's important to discuss the various marketing strategies that you'll implement to keep brand awareness relevant.

This can include distributing flyers, offering promotional discounts to new customers for referrals, and of course, various online campaigns advertised on your website and social media pages. Since much of your marketing will be done online, it's crucial to highlight how you'll do this. You can also mention specific platforms and offer examples of where online marketing has been successful for other boba shops.

8. Organizational Plan

Identifying the staff who will be working in your boba shop is an equally important part of your business plan.

- **Business organization:** Draw up an organogram, identifying the different employees who will work in the front section, kitchen, as well as administrative staff. In some instances, there may only be you and a partner in the early days, or you may have the budget in place to employ a few more employees.
- **Organizational budget:** The organizational budget refers to the cost you're expecting to pay on salaries.

9. Financial Plan

This section is where you discuss financial planning and aspirations in more detail.

- **Underlying assumptions:** How much do you anticipate your business to grow per year? What do you base this information on?
- **Financial highlights:** The financial highlights of your business will always be to show positive cash flow and profitability in each year of operation.
- **Sensitivity analysis:** How will your business remain profitable? The answer is, usually, by keeping pricing relatively low within industry standards and enforcing active marketing campaigns.
- **Source of funds:** A breakdown of the funds. How much is from the anticipated loan or investment and how much you as the owner will be putting into the business?
- **Referencing:** List the various sources you used to gather your information. This will include websites that portray statistics relevant to your marketing plans as well as figures and calculations that show the successes of similar businesses in the bubble tea industry.

Key Takeaways

- A detailed business plan is essential to creating an organized business.
- Add as much detail to the business plan as is relevant—be concise and accurate.
- Include graphs, tables, and any other relevant criteria to illustrate the key aspects of your boba shop business.
- List marketing campaigns in detail, and where possible, include sources and examples of instances where these types of campaigns have worked.

Chapter 5:

BubbleTeaology

Equipment and Supplies

Traditionally, very little equipment was used to create great-tasting bubble tea. This might be your argument when it comes to deciding which bubble tea machines are must-haves versus the ones that can be considered nice-to-haves. However, the reality is that with so many boba stores popping up all over the place, you must decide if you want to give your business the best chance to succeed or if you just want to serve mediocre boba tea. Imagine for a second if a franchise such as Starbucks was making coffee using just a regular kettle. For starters, there'd be no consistency in the quality or flavor of the product produced. The same can be said for your boba tea.

Secondly, imagine trying to manually make boba tea for a stream of morning customers passing by your shop on their way to work. Sounds a little chaotic to me! It's this train of thought that led me to get into the commercial bubble tea machine aspect of the industry. In my years in Taiwan, I found that many people were using sub-standard machinery and supplies, which obviously affected the quality of the boba they were producing. One thing became very clear to me—and that was that if you want your boba business to not only succeed but thrive and outsell your competitors, you need quality, commercial-grade machinery.

Commercial Bubble Tea Machines Worth Considering

Investing in quality machinery and supplies may seem like a hefty investment in the initial stages of your boba journey. However, with so many other aspects of your bubble tea business that you need to focus on, why not opt for the perfect machinery from the get-go? In the process, you'll be checking the most crucial box on your to-do list—making superior boba!

If you're serious about making your mark in the boba business, here's a list of the machinery that you need to help you do it:

1. Bubble Teacup Sealing Machine

We've all, at some point in our lives, ordered a drink from a takeout place and ended up with a flimsy cup that spills more of the drink than it holds. The last thing you want is for customers to pass on your boba because it's messy. Furthermore, a messy drink looks unprofessional. It's for this reason that I always recommend every boba entrepreneur invest in a sealer machine that's designed to handle a boba teacup.

Benefits of a Bubble Teacup Sealing Machine

- boasts a sealing capacity of 500 cups per hour
- easily seals PET, PP, and paper cup options
- since the unit is compact, it requires very little counter space and can easily stand near the Point-of-Sale terminal on the front counter
- easy to clean and simple to operate
- Sealing is done with a roll of film which takes up considerably less storage space than boxes of plastic lids.
- One roll of film can easily seal about 3,900 cups and in most cases is cheaper than plastic lids.
- Seals can also be customized to feature your brand logo.

2. Boba Tea Brewer

The first step in making the perfect cup of boba is without a doubt brewing the right tea. Opting for a boba tea brewer will ensure that you get a superior cup of bubble tea every time. All you need to do is add the desired type of tea–green, black, and oolong–and the machine will do the rest.

Benefits of a tea brewer

- USB programming capable
- pre-infusion and pulse brew creates maximum flavor extraction
- digital displays can be programmed to show specific advertising messages
- simple pulse display for easy programming
- process is simple and easily reduces any astringent tea taste
- creates a consistent quality of tea, every time— this means that any of your employees can create a great-tasting boba drink
- product wastage is minimized as you place the required amounts into the machine
- easy to clean—a huge plus in a busy boba shop

3. Bubble Tea Shaker

Evenly mixed ingredients are the key to creating a consistent, flavorful bubble tea drink. This applies to traditional boba as well as any designer recipes you might be keen on introducing to your menu. Despite exotic flavors and bright colors, your customers are first and foremostly expecting a perfectly blended cup of tea.

Perfecting this manually takes some skill and can be time-consuming to teach to every employee. With a machine, the process is as simple as adding the ingredients and pushing a button!

Benefits of a Bubble Tea Shaker

- Its compact design makes it easy to store on a counter in your commercial kitchen.
- Opting for the Dasin model will afford you the luxury of 10 speeds and five custom programs, making this unit one of the more advanced models currently available.
- Both plastic and stainless-steel shaker cups can be used because the unit features adjustable arms that ensure the cup fits snugly—suitable for 500ml or 700ml cups.
- It's easy to clean and simple to operate.

4. Automatic Bubble Tea Fructose Dispenser

Any boba drinker will tell you that customizing your favorite drink is all about adding the right amount of syrup to the tea blend. Too much can make your tea too sweet while too little may leave it tasting bland. Rather than try to manually get each recipe combination right for each recipe, why not invest in a bubble tea fructose dispenser?

Benefits of an Automatic Bubble Tea Fructose Dispenser

- dispenses correct proportions of bubble tea syrup, making it ideal for customizing designer boba drinks
- reduces employee training costs because there's no need to learn different sweetness levels manually
- operation is simple and quick to learn
- easy to clean

5. Automatic Tapioca Pearl Boba Cooker

Many boba tea entrepreneurs will agree: The hardest part of the whole bubble tea brewing process is mastering the art of making the perfect tapioca pearls. Why struggle with pots and pans when you can use a machine that's been designed to consistently make the best tapioca pearls? Since this machine has been designed to make the perfect tapioca pearls, you can be assured of complete consistency, every time!

Benefits of a Tapioca Pearl Boba Cooker

- It's the quickest way to produce fresh, consistent results.

- The unit is stainless steel, ensuring quality and durability.
- It automatically sets the temperature, boils water, and even stirs tea. By cutting down on employee costs, this machine is amazing value for money.
- It boasts four different temperature sensors throughout the pot and creates accurate cooking.
- It is easy to operate, meaning that anyone can make tapioca pearls whenever needed—no need to rely on a designated employee.

It's also important to note that this machine may not be a common accessory in many boba stores. The reason for this is that many boba entrepreneurs opt for pre-packaged boba. By opting to use this machine, you will really make your store stand out as a bubble tea shop that makes boba fresh (it's even something you could advertise on your website and social pages)!

Choosing the Right Cups

Choosing the right bubble teacup is essential to ensuring you present the tea in a manner that's both professional and appealing. While your goal might be to do things a little differently from your competitors, the right cup is one of the boba basics that you absolutely must get right from the very beginning.

- **PP cups:** Essentially, the most common boba cups are PP cups, which are available in 12oz (360ml), 16oz (500ml), and 24 oz (700ml). PP plastic cups are usually 95mm in size and are the most common type of plastic for boba and other drinks. This is usually because this type of material is the least expensive.

- **PET plastic:** For a harder, clearer plastic cup, you might opt for PET. It's usually 98mm in size and creates the impression of being more expensive. They're a popular choice in high-end boba stores and are generally more expensive than PP cups. In case you're wondering, Starbucks uses PET cups—that should give you an idea of the basic differences between them and PP cups.

- **Paper cups:** One of the top concerns many people have with boba stores is the excessive use of plastic and its impact on the environment. The good news is that by offering a paper cup alternative, you can reduce your brand's carbon footprint. The paper cups used by boba stores are usually about 90mm and can easily be customized with your logo. They can also be sealed as easily as a plastic cup.

- **PLA cups:** If you're looking for the most biodegradable option on the market, PLA cups might be what you're looking for. For the most part, these cups are made with corn and can be easily recycled. They are 96mm in size, and while they aren't ideal for hot coffee temperatures, they're ideal for colder tea options.

Are Custom Cups Pricey?

When you're starting in the boba business, your first thought might be to use non-branded cups to save costs. What you might not know is that custom cups cost around $.06 per cup, which in some cases is the same or very close to clear cups. I'll highlight a few top reasons to rather invest in branded supplies from day one in Chapter 6.

Another point to keep in mind with ordering cups is that most vendors have a minimum order quantity (MOQ), which means you might have to order between 10–20 boxes each time. With this in mind, it's important to know exactly what cups you want to use as well as what logo you're going to use. If you're not sure, I recommend going to your local grocery store and buying one packet of each cup type to test your boba in. Compare how each option looks and how it portrays your brand. Alternatively, if you want your brand to be associated with sustainability, then paper cups are the way to go from the beginning!

Straws—What's the Fuss About?

By now, you will have realized that the right straw is as crucial to the boba drinking experience as the tapioca pearls. Straws that are used for boba drinks need to be thicker than your average soda straw. Of course, this is so that you can easily suck up the tapioca and chew the pearls as you enjoy drinking the tea. Traditionally, boba straws are the plastic types that you might associate with being served with some types of milkshakes. However, with the recent emphasis on the ban on single-use plastic in some areas, where does that leave your need for thousands of straws?

Fortunately, paper straws are making a considerable impact on the market. While they were once flimsy, the good news is that they have become stronger and more durable. This makes them the perfect alternative to plastic straws. More good news is that BubbleTealogy has overcome the issue with the flat sides by creating an angled edge on one side. That means you can easily pierce the film on your Boba tea without struggling or making a mess. I recommend that you always ensure that the straws you want to order are compatible with your type of sealer film.

Choosing the Right Vendor

When you're pricing your materials, you might find that some vendors are cheaper with certain items but more costly with others. This may lead you to consider buying supplies from various vendors. Also, consider how time-consuming this will be and how this affects your business in the long run. Where possible, choose a vendor that can supply you with all (or a great deal of) the necessary supplies. In many instances, having one general supplier will simplify the ordering process. You may also qualify for bulk discounts and ordering promotions of these are available.

Furthermore, if there are shipping costs involved, one order equals one shipping fee, or in some instances, free shipping. Don't be fooled into thinking you're saving money on a product because it's cheaper, but in the end, you're paying an exorbitant shipping fee. Another advantage of using one vendor is that you won't receive your products in dribs and drabs.

Additional Benefits to Look Out for When Choosing a Supplier

To take some strain off your budget, companies, such as BubbleTealogy, offer free shipping to the continental US. Furthermore, we offer a 1-year warranty on all our machines as well as the training material to help you get your employees trained in the process of using the machines. Always compare this to other companies that you might be considering, ensuring that you're getting the best value for your money.

Bubble Tea Equipment Certification

When choosing the best bubble tea-making equipment, it's imperative to ensure that all the machines have the necessary certification. For the most part, US and Canadian laws dictate that all machinery be UL or UL EPH, or NSF Certified. This will always depend on the health department regulations in your area, so be sure to verify this before ordering any equipment locally from international vendors.

Key Takeaways

- There are a variety of bubble tea-making machines that will streamline the boba-making processes in your shop.
- Choosing a reputable bubble tea machine supplier, such as BubbleTeaology, will provide you with quality products that are compact and user-friendly.
- Choosing the right cup is as important as choosing the right ingredients.
- Always opt for a vendor that can supply you with all the required supplies, as this will help you create an efficient ordering process, as well as save you costs in the long run.

- While using single-use plastic is becoming frowned upon, the good news is that there are environmentally-friendly paper options for the disposable aspects of your products.
- Check the equipment certification in your area before ordering any machines—you can do this by consulting your local health department's regulations.

Chapter 6:

Unique Branding Ideas

When it comes to branding, you might be of two minds about the general concept. I've had potential boba business owners who only want to brand their stores and not their cups. Then, I've had eager entrepreneurs who want to brand everything that has anything to do with their boba business. Well, to be honest, I'm inclined to side with the second group of bubble tea business owners. If something can be branded, it should be. Simple as that.

Branding is an integral part of making your boba business successful. Aside from looking professional, branding also helps potential customers identify your product with you and your business. If setting up your boba business is your first real exposure to the business world, then it's important to understand why there's so much emphasis on branding. In this chapter, I'll cover the following:

- creating an Engaging and Relatable Brand

- the top Reasons Why Your Boba Shop Needs a Powerful Logo

- tips for creating the perfect logo

- tips for designing the perfect bubble tea shop menu

Creating an Engaging and Relatable Brand

I need to emphasize an important point before we go any further: Branding is about a lot more than creating a catchy logo. Essentially, your brand is made up of all the aspects that make you stand out from your competitors. This includes everything from a great product to a noteworthy customer experience. When you ask a stranger in the street what they think of your product, what do you want them to say? Would they respond with joy and excitement at the thought of great service and a wonderful-tasting product, or will they frown and not be impressed?

It's no secret that branding requires very careful planning and implementation to make it effective. I've included a few guidelines to assist you in creating an engaging and relatable boba brand.

1. **Cater to your niche:** The good news here is that you've already identified your niche market, also referred to as your target audience. That said, it makes starting the branding process considerably easier if you know beforehand who you're targeting. You won't waste any resources trying to identify who enjoys your product! On average, your target audiences are

Millennials and Gen Zers aged between 20 and 29.

2. **Highlight what makes you different:** You might think it's difficult to highlight what makes you different if you're selling a product that is currently all the rage. There are, however, a few factors that differentiate you from your competitors. These are:

- creating vision and mission statements that are unique and personal to you

- a unique approach to serving and selling a readily available product

- a customer experience that's unique to your boba shop (that includes the general vibe and ambiance of your store and staff)

3. **Introduce your brand to your community:** A top way to create an engaging brand is by getting involved in charity events in your community. Not only will you show potential customers that your brand is interested in supporting local projects, but it will also put a face to the brand. Consumers are more likely to support your brand if they feel as if they know the people behind it.

4. **Create a high-quality website and blog:** In the digital world, it has become crucial to interact with people where they hang out—and

that's online. Creating an interactive website that shows your products and brand values is only one rung on the branding ladder. You'll also need an interactive blog that enables you to communicate issues about your brand. For instance, a boba blog should have content related to your products and the health benefits of boba drinks. Content should be relevant and engaging with colorful images of your products.

5. **Add your branding:** Aside from branding being about the customer experience, it's also about the actual product and the images such as logos and slogans that potential customers can associate with your particular boba tea products. If you're not going to purchase a franchise, you will have to design your own logo. Let's dive into a few reasons why you need a logo.

Top Reasons Why Your Boba Shop Needs a Powerful Logo

In your boba business, chances are that the bulk of your customers will leave with your product in their hands. If they're walking to the office or school, they'll possibly walk past many other people (or even as they sit on the train or bus). This means that many people could potentially see the cups in their hands. And, if the colorful drink inside looks appealing with tapioca pearls floating in the bottom (because you opted for clear cups), consider what a great advert that is for your shop! Furthermore, if the passersby can see your store name or logo, they will definitely know where to find that tasty-looking beverage. Right there you have effective advertising you didn't pay for!

Aside from some free advertising, there are a bunch of other good reasons why you need a powerful logo on everything associated with your boba shop.

1. Create a Foundation for Your Brand Identity

First and foremost, successful branding tells the story of your business. Its goal is to influence potential customers' emotions and serve to remind them why they need a cup or two of your boba every day. Moreover, a business's logo design is the foundation on which your brand is created. When a customer sees your logo, they should automatically associate it with your product and your brand's story.

2. Logos Grab Attention

Did you know that your brand has an average of two seconds to create an impression on a potential customer? If potential customers aren't familiar with your product, they will base their first impression on how effective your branding is at grabbing their attention. Again, think of the customer on the bus, holding their tea. A plain white cup won't draw as much attention as a branded cup. Have you ever seen a Starbucks cup? Their simple green logo is so popular that it's even recognized by people who don't drink coffee. Never owned a pair of Nike's? Yet, you know what the logo looks like, don't you? Don't own a

Ferrari? I'll bet you'll instantly recognize a Ferrari logo! The same can be said for hundreds of other logos.

3. Differentiates You From the Competition

While the business model for a boba shop is pretty standard, there are nuances in each brand and store that make it unique. For instance, you could choose to specialize in designer boba rather than the more traditional options. How will a potential customer know that without entering your store? What tells a new customer that you're not "just another bubble tea shop?" Your logo (and/or slogan) is your way of telling people that you're not only different from your competitors, but considerably better!

4. Creates and Sustains Brand Loyalty

Something you'll learn very quickly as you launch your boba shop is that consumers not only *want* but actually *crave* consistency. That's why people will brave the cold and the long lines to get a cup of coffee at Starbucks. People want to align themselves with brands they enjoy and feel confident in. So, as your boba brand becomes more familiar to a larger range of customers, this familiarity will grow into loyalty. Aside from a great-tasting product, a well-designed logo assists in building brand loyalty.

Tips to Create the Perfect Logo

When it's time to create your logo, you might be tempted to use your favorite image or clip art. You may also want to use as much color as possible to attract attention and use the curliest font to be different from everyone else. You might be surprised to learn that none of these tactics will help you create an effective logo. If you're creating your own logo, the tips below might come in handy:

1. **Choose the right image**: Ever heard the expression, "A picture paints a thousand words"? Well, it's never been more accurate than in relation to an effective logo. To be clear, your logo is a visual representation of your boba brand—It's easier to *show* people what your bubble tea business is about rather than trying to convey it in a few sentences. That said, choose a simple image or icon that people will be able to easily relate to. For instance, just about every boba business uses a tea glass in their logos. If you're going to do the same, find a unique but simple way to do it.

2. **Use white space:** Your logo is going to be on the front of your cups, napkins, t-shirts, and even your store window. This means when designing your logo, you don't want it to be cluttered. It should be easily recognizable. Potential customers should be able to read your

logo on both small and big surfaces. Designers recommend leaving adequate blank space (also called white space) around the logo to ensure that it doesn't get cluttered.

3. **Utilize color effectively**: Designing your logo isn't an opportunity to stash all your favorite colors into one small space at once. Experiment with a few colors but be sure to not overdo it. Too many colors will detract from the message you're trying to share—that you sell great boba!

4. **Use a legible font:** Use a font that people can read. If you're going to use a slogan with your logo, be sure to use a clean font that's easy to read from a distance and at any size. Your customers shouldn't have to squint to try and read it.

Tips for Designing the Perfect Bubble Tea Shop Menu

In your boba shop, your menu is a visual representation of your brand and the products on offer. Your menu design should express your brand's personality as well as exude quality and professionalism. It's important to note that there's no real right or wrong method to creating a menu—what works in some shops might not work in others. However, there are a few clear guidelines that will get you on the right track.

Let's take a look at the most significant tips to make menu creation much easier:

1. **Keep it simple**: Colors and fonts should be simple, easy to read, and shouldn't be overwhelming. Be sure to use a color and font combination that matches the theme and color of your brand logo. Your brand looks more professional if your menu and branding are a mirror image of one another.

2. **Include descriptions:** While you might know what's inside an oolong boba drink, the average person entering your store for the first time most likely won't. It's always a good idea to add a short description under each product.

3. **Don't crowd your menu:** You might think that the best way to succeed in the bubble tea business is to fill your menu with as many tea options as possible. This can, however, be too overwhelming for your customers, especially if they are new to the whole boba experience. Instead, focus on an average of 10–15 items and divide them into categories. Common categories include:

   - **Fresh Tea:** (List the tea options such as black tea, green tea, chamomile tea, and even honey green tea)

   - **Bubble Milk Tea:** (bubble tea made with fresh milk–list the types you offer such as coconut, peppermint, strawberry, or oolong)

- **Fruit Infused Tea:** Fruity flavored boba–list the options such as strawberry green tea, lemon green tea, and passion fruit green tea.

4. Smoothies: List the options on offer such as banana, matcha, strawberry, taro, and coconut.

5. Differentiate ingredient levels: Since sugar, milk, and ice are a matter of preference, it's important to provide your customer with options. For instance, specify that customers can choose between "no sugar, a little sugar, regular sugar" or "no ice, regular ice, or extra ice." You also want to highlight that there are various milk options available for people who don't drink dairy. Popular options such as soy, oats, or even almond are general favorites with bubble tea customers.

6. Make prices visible: Prices should be displayed clearly next to each item. For the most part, boba shops offer two options—medium-sized cups (500ml or 16oz) and a larger option (700ml or 24oz).

7. Add optional extras: Bubble tea drinks can be served straight up or with an assortment of toppings. If you're offering toppings (such as fruit or jelly pieces), be sure to list them separately under a different category. As with toppings on food menus, these are usually priced per serving. Boba toppings usually vary between $1,00 and $1.50. Again, this would vary according to the type of topping and its availability.

8. Pricing: There isn't an industry standard for pricing bubble tea drinks. Each store does its pricing based on the ingredients and required profit margins. Google competitors' menus and visit other boba stores in the same area to get an idea of what they're serving and at what prices. Availability of ingredients may also play a part in certain price calculations.

9. Offer side items: It's a good idea to offer a few extras to boost your revenue. It's also a good way to add variety to your menu. Popular sides include ice cream, bubble waffles, and even Taiwanese snow ice (also known as shaved ice). You can also include a few snack items popular to the area as a way to attract new customers.

Branding Through Employee Uniforms

Another effective way to get your brand out there is to ensure that you design shirts, t-shirts, or even polo shirts for all your employees. Have a local workwear company embroider or print your logo onto the shirts. Not only will your employees look professional, but this will also show customers that you take your brand seriously enough to design uniforms for your staff. Furthermore, everyone your employee passes on the way to and from work will see your logo. And who better to answer questions about the brand and its products than the professional wearing the shirt?

If you're going to be sending someone to hand out leaflets around town or even the bus or train station, it's a good idea to give them a branded shirt to wear–that will already attract potential customer attention.

Key Takeaways

- Creating a relatable brand is important for marketing your boba business.
- Use your brand to cater to your niche—which is selling bubble tea.
- Your brand should always highlight the factors that make your business different.
- Create an interactive website and blog with relevant content to engage with potential and existing consumers.
- An effective logo creates a foundation for effective identity.
- My website has a logo-creating function that will help you get the right logo for your business—be sure to check it out!

Chapter 7:

Hiring and Training

Employees

No matter how hands-on you are, there are two crucial factors you should understand from the get-go. The first is that you won't be able to run your boba shop on your own. There's simply too much to be done! Some of the tasks that need doing on a single day include making delicious boba, checking online orders for pick-ups, ordering stock, answering the phone, taking payments, working on your marketing, keeping the store and kitchen clean, and, of course, engaging with your customers. Trying to do everything on your own will either result in you suffering from burnout or you neglecting one of these crucial duties, which, in turn, will seriously hamper the success of your boba store.

The other factor that you need to understand is that the right employees are your business's most valuable asset. While it's true that the unemployment rate is up and hiring people is easier than ever, you should approach your boba plan with the intent of hiring quality staff who will grow your business to its intended goals. If this will be your first time hiring or dealing with employees, there are a few pointers and tips that I'd like to share with you.

Why Are Staff Your Most Valuable Asset?

Your staff are the face of your business. When consumers walk into your store, the employee they interact with first creates their general impression of your whole business. Friendly, helpful staff who provide good service create a sense of professionalism, and your consumer will want to buy your boba. With so many bubble tea businesses popping up, it's not difficult for consumers to find a shop that can give them what they need. Hiring the right employees are key to ensuring that your customers (and general visitors to your store) receive the best experience possible. More to the point, how you treat your staff will impact the way they treat your customers.

How to Find the Right Boba Shop Employees (Cashiers, Admin Staff, Cleaners, and Kitchen Assistants)

It's no secret that the food and beverages industry has the largest staff turnover in the US. Essentially, the main reason for this is that restaurant and cafe owners are more likely to employ the wrong types of people in the first place. The second reason is a lack of proper industry-related training. Take your boba business, for instance. For the most part, you're serving customers tea. Does this mean anyone can do it? Making tea at home is considerably different from serving a top-notch boba drink. With that in mind, here are some crucial tips to ensure you hire the right employees from the start:

1. The Right Attitude

It has to be said: The right attitude makes all the difference in business. This is especially true in situations where you're dealing with people. Employing people with can-do attitudes ensures that tasks are completed proactively and in a timely manner. Look for people who want to be part of a successful team. Whether they're the cleaner or the manager, the right attitude is key to their intended role.

2. Employ a Personality

While the boba industry may be fairly simple to master in a very short time, not everyone is cut out to work with people in a cafe setting. There's no point in hiring a shy person to greet patrons at the door. That employee will always feel uncomfortable and will eventually leave. Your employees should have beaming, vivacious personalities, and they should be able to easily strike up conversations with customers. Employees with the right personalities will also be able to diffuse confrontational situations before they escalate. They will also be able to encourage sales and repeat business.

3. Check Reliability

The last thing you want in your business is to have to deal with unreliable staff. Staff who don't show up for work not only create additional pressure for the other employees but also make it seem as though your business is understaffed. This results in long lines and irate patrons who may choose to not return. Check potential employees' reliability with their previous employers before hiring them.

4. Hire Skills

Many new business owners shy away from hiring employees with too much skill or experience. This is usually because skill comes with a higher price tag. However, never underestimate the benefits of hiring staff with experience and skills of working in a boba shop! Not only will they already be familiar with the environment, but they may be able to assist with the training of new employees.

How to Find the Right Boba Barista

While all job functions in your boba shop are important, let's face it: The person making the boba drinks is the person you rely on the most to make your dream of being a successful bubble shop owner come true! In fact, something I've seen a lot in Taiwanese bubble tea shops is that customers won't mind standing in a long line to have their favorite boba barista make their tea just the way they like it.

After all, it's a bubble tea shop's first and foremost priority, and if the boba is awesome, people will be lining up. Longer lines equal more revenue. So, yes, your boba barista needs to be both professional and skilled. With that in mind, just how do you go about finding the best boba barista for your business?

1. Know What You Want

By the time you start interviewing potential boba baristas, you should have an idea of what you want them to do. Will they only need to prepare the boba or will you need them to help where needed? Would you prefer them to already have bubble tea-making experience, or will there be adequate time for training and testing? How many hours will they be required to work? What personality traits are you looking for?

I recommend always looking for a boba barista with some experience in the bubble tea industry. Additionally, they should have a teachable attitude and excellent communication skills. Keep in mind that there won't be time for on-the-job training for your barista, as consumers expect you to offer the best quality products from day one.

2. Ask the Right Questions

Refrain from asking open-ended questions to which the answers are either yes or no. This won't give you much insight into the applicant's personality and aspirations. You need to assess if the candidate is looking for an in-between job until something better comes along or if they're serious about the position. Ideally, you don't want to be training a new barista even for a few months. Pay particular attention to the way they talk about their previous job. This will tell you a lot about the type of person they are and give you some insight into their work ethic.

3. Follow-up On Previous Employment

Recommendations are often not an accurate representation of the person you're interviewing. After all, would a candidate list any employer who would give them a bad review? However, phoning the previous company and speaking to someone other than the specific person listed may give you insight into the following:

- their ability to follow instructions, as well as their openness to be a part of new training

- ability to deal with customer or staff conflict

- communication levels

- time management

4. Test Your Candidates

If the success of your boba shop depends on the quality of the product you're providing to customers, then you must experience the boba from that perspective. Once you've shortlisted potential candidates, have a testing session with each one. Don't ask them to make a boba they're good at creating. Rather, ask them to prepare two or three options from your preliminary menu, as if you were a customer. Observe the following:

- Does the applicant demonstrate knowledge of industry-specific skills, such as the correct way to cook tapioca?

- Can they work under pressure? (This will be a valuable skill when the breakfast line is building up in the front of your store)

- Do they know how to assemble the finished drink?

- How long does it take them to do this?

How to Find the Right Management for Your Boba Shop

As the owner of the boba business, it may not always be possible for you to be in the store the whole day to supervise and assist with the day-to-day running of things. This means it might be necessary to employ a store manager. Since this person will be in a more senior position than your other employees, it may be necessary to apply a different selection criterion.

Essentially, your boba store manager should have previous experience in a manager role, preferably in the food and beverage industry. This is to ensure that everything gets off on a stable and organized footing. As your business progresses, key individuals within the store can be identified and trained as potential managers. A few pointers to consider include the following:

- **Can create the right culture:** Opt for a person who can create an engaging and motivating culture within your boba store—this culture must blend in with your brand and business goals.
- **Manage staff issues:** Experience with managing staff in a cafe or boba shop setting (this will include dealing with employee issues such as late coming and absenteeism).
- **Oversee daily operations:** The right manager will ensure that the normal day-to-day store operations run smoothly and will be able to deal with all aspects of the business, such as setting daily sales targets, cash-ups, staff issues, customer complaints, product ordering, and upholding required health and safety standards.
- **Training and selection:** Part of a manager's duties will be to ensure that routine training sessions are held for existing staff, as well as training being held for new employees.
- **Set up staff schedules:** Create and implement effective staff schedules.

The Importance of Ongoing Training Within Your Boba Environment

Training is as crucial in your boba shop as it is in any other type of business. It's crucial to provide your employees with the following training to ensure that your shop runs as professionally as you need it to:

1. **Product training:** This type of training revolves around the types of products you'll be selling and how they're made. Understanding the terminology and processes will enable your staff to answer customer questions accurately and professionally. For instance, a consumer asking what the black balls in the boba are shouldn't be met with a shrug or a "who knows?" expression. Rather, employees should be able to explain what the ingredients are and where they're from.

2. **History of the product:** Since bubble tea is all the rage right now, consumers are naturally curious about its origins and how it came about. Employees should know the basics. That way, they can easily interact with customers.

3. **Machine training:** Whether you're going to have one bubble tea maker or you're opting for the full range to simplify your boba processes, employees should know how they work.

4. **POS training:** All employees in the store should know how to process a receipt. Having only one person with skills in how to use the POS system will leave you in a tight spot when that person is off sick or busy with a customer query at the other end of the store.

5. **Product storage:** Everyone should know the proper procedures for storing both open and sealed ingredients. This will ensure that the kitchen is clean at all times, as well as ensuring that stock storage is within the health department guidelines at all times.

6. **Customer service:** Ensure that all employees have received training on how to deal with customer queries as well as how to de-escalate a tense situation between a customer and a fellow employee. While you may think there are no customer service issues in a tea shop, the reality is, if there are customers and products, there will always be the risk of customer queries. Improving customer service should be part of ongoing training.

7. **Brand awareness:** Employees should know about the brand they work for. This includes who the owners are, the history of the brand, what the brand stands for, as well as the business goals. If your business is involved in local charity events, this is something that your employees should be able to tell interested customers about. They should also be able to

refer customers to your social media platforms and recommend they post stories and photos about their experience in the store and with the brand.

Tips for Making Bubble Tea Training Fun

Some people may argue with me on the following point, but I believe that training should be fun—that is, if you want it to be effective. Fortunately, working in a boba shop isn't complex and your staff won't require extreme sessions of constant training. It is, however, necessary to have weekly, monthly, or quarterly sessions to refresh the staff on brand values such as customer service and conflict resolution. These sessions are also the perfect time to brainstorm with your staff about potential menu changes, additions, and even promotional ideas.

You might think that you'll have enough things to do without having to worry over "soft" training for employees. It is, however, crucial to make the effort, as your employees will either create your success or lead to your shop's demise. The last thing you need to be dealing with is a series of customer complaints over bad service. To make the training process easier, follow these simple steps:

1. **Create a staff training plan:** Draw up a register listing the type of training each specific job function should know. For instance, everybody might not need to know how to make bubble tea, but everyone should know how to interact with customers professionally.

2. **Use the buddy system:** Assign each new employee to an existing employee who you know will show them the ropes. Test the new employees' understanding of what they're learning.

3. **Hands-on training is best:** Don't just explain what you want employees to do. Show them and let them role-play what they've learned. In an environment where there is so much competition, it's very easy for a customer to walk away from your business if they aren't assisted by a competent employee.

4. **Have pop quizzes:** It's important to highlight menu or ingredient changes with staff, as they need to explain these changes to customers. Have regular pop quizzes with your staff to ensure they can answer customer questions about any changes.

Tips for Drawing Up Effective Work Schedules

Another reason why both the restaurant and bubble tea industries often see a high employee turnover has to do with inconsistent or overstrained work schedules. Depending on the location of your store, you might need to trade outside the usual nine-to-five scope. For instance, if your store is located on the way to the train station, you'd get a lot more foot traffic if you opened at five or six in the morning to "catch" the morning rush traffic that's heading to the station. In that instance, an early opening time and a later closing time may be more beneficial to your scenario. That said, it might be necessary to draw up a work schedule. I've listed a few tips for doing this:

- **Consider your boba shop's peak times:** The general practice in the first month of trade would be to assess your business's peak times. This will form the backbone of your scheduling structure. During busy times, it may be necessary to have all-hands-on-deck, to ensure business flows smoothly.

- **Determine how many staff members you'll need:** The size of your store, location, and whether or not you'll be serving food will determine how many employees you'll need on each shift. It's a good idea to have two extra employees on each shift in case someone calls in sick. Doing this means there's always someone to wipe down tables and stock fridges if necessary. Having two people who know how to expertly make boba on each shift is a good idea to ensure you aren't left short-staffed in an emergency.

- **Consider employee input into the schedule:** As you and your store manager draw up the schedules, it's always a good idea to consider employee input into the schedules. Involving your employees will make them more willing to work longer hours.

Each boba shop is unique and you will have to evaluate your store's specific needs. Smaller spaces might only require one barista, and the hours might be manageable enough for you to just need one team of employees. When evaluating what works for your store, be sure to review your local labor laws to avoid non-compliance. Additionally, you need to ensure your staff members have adequate time off and stick to the regulations regarding overtime and weekly work hours.

Payroll Software for Independent Boba Shop Owners

The most efficient way to ensure that your employee salaries are calculated correctly is by using a reliable payroll software system. Ideally, you want to choose an option that's been specifically designed for the coffee and/or tea shop environment. The good news is that there are several popular options to choose from. I've listed some of these to help you in the selection process:

- SurePayroll
- OnPay Payroll
- Inova Payroll
- Square Payroll
- Wave Payroll

POS Software for Independent Boba Shops

If you're going to be setting your boba shop up independently (without a franchise), it's crucial to have the correct POS system in place to ensure that there are no hiccups at a key point in your business. Having the right POS software in place will also make it easier for your employees to give your customers the service they're paying for. As you review potential POS options, consider the following pointers:

- **Features:** Businesses have come a long way from those heavy, clunky registers of days gone by. And thank goodness for it! Modern POS (point-of-sale) systems promote store efficiency with a user-friendly interface. Additionally, you can opt for systems specially designed for coffee and/or tea shops that simplify the receipting process. Always look for systems that boast features that can enhance your service to your customers. Some of these include inventory management, sales tracking capabilities, and customer profile tools.

- **Efficiency:** No business owner wants to be using a system that can't keep up with the long breakfast line in a busy boba shop. Always opt for a POS that's super easy to use and doesn't require a lot of steps to go from placing an order to the actual payment.

- **Contract fees:** The prices of POS systems are as extensive as the boba drinks your store will be serving! That means it will take some research on your part to choose the option best suited to your business needs. Some systems require a one-off payment, while others have additional monthly contracts and fees. To save money in the long run, you should compare prices, contracts, and features. Remember to include the price of this system in your business plan if you're going to be requesting financial assistance from a lender or investor.

- **Vendor customer service:** A working POS is a central point in any bubble tea shop. Therefore, any issues with the equipment can lead to downtime in your shop, as well as a loss of sales and potential customers. Be sure to do accurate research on the customer service offered by the vendor you're purchasing the system from. You need to know that your staff will get the assistance they need to be able to serve customers as efficiently as possible.

POS Software Options

Quite possibly the biggest advantage to using an effective POS is how it streamlines your business. It's also a terrific tool to ensure that your staff provides the service that can set your shop apart from other bubble tea businesses. A few POS options that seem to be quite common in the bubble tea industry are:

- ShopKeep iPad POS
- Toast POS
- Lightspeed POS
- NCR Aloha
- Lavu
- Revel Systems
- Clover Station
- Loyverse
- Square

PayRoll Taxes

No matter where you set up your business, there will be certain tax laws that need to be upheld when it comes to employee salaries. It's important to check with your local tax office to learn what the criteria is. Ensure that your payroll software is set up as per these tax requirements. Be sure to keep records of all tax-related documents for the business as well as all employees.

Key Takeaways

- Never forget that staff are your most valuable asset.
- Create interview criteria for the employee positions you want in your boba shop.
- Do thorough interviews based on what your shop needs.
- Boba baristas should have experience in the bubble tea industry.
- Employees should be adequately trained in all aspects of your shop.
- Draw up work schedules based on your store's unique traffic.
- Invest in payroll and POS software to streamline your business process.
- Check the employee tax rates with the local tax office.

Chapter 8:

Growing Your New

Business

Since the bubble tea business is booming, you will have a considerable amount of competition. Because boba is a simple product, it can easily be added to any existing restaurant or cafe's menu. That means you'll be competing against boba shops as well as potentially well-known food businesses that may exist in the area. With that said, you're going to have to pull out the big guns when it comes to creating an effective marketing strategy.

Fortunately, there are several fun and innovative ways to approach your marketing strategy. With a bit of out-of-the-box thinking, there's no reason why your boba shop can't be as lucrative and popular as the top bubble tea shops currently sharing the industry.

Bubble Tea Promotion/Sales Generating Ideas

I've compiled a few strategy suggestions to get you started. For many boba entrepreneurs, these are the basics. And the message here is—get the basics right and the rest of your business will fall into place.

Strategy #1: Create a Comprehensive and Engaging Website

It's almost a given that every business these days has a website. When searching for your brand, your website will be the first thing potential customers search for. Aside from showcasing hundreds of images of your delicious boba drinks, customers can also use your website to leave or read reviews. Additionally, if your website is professionally created, you will be able to generate free traffic from search engines and lead potential customers to your social media pages.

If you've never created your own website before, you should consider outsourcing it to a professional (such as a digital marketing service). That way, they can optimize it and add the relevant SEO content which, in turn, will help you get traffic to your site. If, however, you want to create your own website, these next few tips may come in handy.

1. Create a website to generate awareness (for everything you add, ask yourself if it will attract traffic or generate sales).

2. Your website must be super easy to navigate, meaning that visitors shouldn't struggle to find what they're looking for.

3. Use original and relevant content—update information regularly.

4. Always use high-quality images—make all the bubble teas on your menu and have a professional photographer take photos of the different options. Potential customers will be more interested in seeing a final product before buying it.

5. Link out to your social media pages—encourage visitors to "like and share" all your pages.

6. Ensure that your website has the correct protocols to ensure that you don't have slow-loading pages or images that won't display correctly. Speeding up your website usually helps with this.

7. Ask friends, family, and employees to access the website from their different devices—that way, you'll know if there's a problem opening links or pages.

8. It's important to ensure that your internal search bar works, making it easy for customers to locate what they're looking for.

Having an interactive website will be worth it in the end as your website will form the basis of your online advertising.

Strategy # 2: Use Social Media to Grow Your Business

Advertising just about anything has never been easier. Courtesy of the digital era, you can launch an incredible amount of advertising without an exorbitant cost. All you need is to create business profiles on various social media platforms and engage and interact with existing and potential customers on a daily or weekly basis. It's as simple as posting quality images of your products and merchandise. Add some interesting content with images of the store and customers enjoying your boba drinks. Additionally, encourage customers to share their experiences and images with their online friends, especially the local ones who can easily visit the store.

If social media is "not really your thing," you either need to brush it off or delegate the task to the store manager. Some of the more popular platforms to advertise your brand and boba on include the following:

- **Instagram:** A brilliant platform for sharing quality images of your various boba drinks. With over two billion users on this platform, it's an excellent place to showcase your brand, product, and shop.

- **Pinterest:** Aside from posting images, Pinterest is terrific for sharing visual content such as blogs on your brand's bubble tea journey. By the end of 2021, the Pinterest platform had an impressive 91 million US users.

- **Facebook:** Since Facebook allows status updates, it's easy to post promotions for the day for loyal customers to see. It's also excellent for advertising a new drink on the menu! Encourage all customers to "like" your Facebook page and share their drinks and experiences. Statistics show that there were 182 million US users on the Facebook platform in 2022, making it the top platform to use to grow your boba brand.

- **Twitter:** With Twitter, you can share store or product news or answer customer questions in real-time. On average, there are 77 million US-based users on the Twitter platform.

- **TikTok:** As the new kid on the block, TikTok is taking the social media environment by storm. You can easily post images, product videos, and live interactions with customers in your store. Include videos of your boba barista making different drinks, customers enjoying your boba products, and current and future promotions. By 2022, TikTok was boasting an average of 80 million US users—60 percent between the ages of 16–24, which ties in quite nicely with the boba tea demographic.

- **YouTube:** Known widely as a platform for user-generated video content, you can create your own channel and post videos about your product and/or brand or store. On average, the US has about 197 million YouTube users.

The golden rule in marketing is to go where your target audience is or hangs out. And these days, that's the internet! So, if you want to make a big difference quickly, launch your boba shop's product profile on as many social platforms as possible. Post images, content, and product specials. Do it often—your demographic "lives" online, and the more content you add, the more relevant your boba products will be to them.

Strategy #3: Sign Up for a Google Business Listing and Get Reviews

The trend these days is to check reviews before going to a new place such as a restaurant, club, or boba shop. After all, people are too busy to waste their time at a mediocre establishment. That said, how will a stranger to your store know you even exist? The answer is simple: you need a Google listing.

Simply set up a Google Business profile at business.google.com. Add photos of the store, products, and related content. Encourage customers to leave a review on the site with a rating. By doing so, you will be listed as part of the attractions in the city and anyone typing in a search for "bubble tea shop" will see your business listing. Encourage visitors to your store to leave an honest review of their experience. In addition to creating awareness, it will also allow you to see how people view your store. You can then also rectify any shortcomings, such as slow service.

Strategy #4: Sign Up for Yelp Reviews

Similar to Google reviews, Yelp also offers a reviewing platform. In fact, it's estimated that Yelp has over 244 million various location reviews, making it the ultimate go-to review site. Generally, 80% of Yelp visitors intend on making a purchase, so if you're listed, you'll most certainly see business from the listing. It's also a good idea to encourage customers to leave a Yelp review, as these are searched online by potential customers or even tourists visiting the area.

Strategy #5: Get Involved With Your Local Community

Another super way to create brand awareness in your local community is to get involved with local events. Many boba entrepreneurs align themselves with charity events that support local causes. Arranging sales booths at farmers' or trade markets is also a popular way to engage with local customers. People in the community will be more likely to support your business if they associate you with these events. Be sure to advertise your presence at these events on all of your social media platforms. Once again, pictures speak louder than words, so be sure to take clear photos of customers and community members enjoying your boba drinks. Post the photos on your website and social platforms. Another good idea would be to print them out and hang them in frames all around your store. Speak to the local community newspaper and ask them if they would be willing to publish a few pictures of the event (believe it or not, not everyone is on the internet!).

Strategy #6: Create a Customer Loyalty Program

Retaining existing business is as important as getting it in the first place. One of the best ways to encourage repeat business is to implement a loyalty program. Offer rewards to the patrons who purchase often, and they'll not only keep returning but also tell people about your store. Once again, be sure to advertise these types of programs on your social media platforms.

Strategy #7: Run Frequent Promotions

Another effective way to get new business is by running frequent promotions. Campaigns such as "two for one," "half-price Monday," and "buy a boba and get an X for free," are just a few ideas you can implement. Encourage your employees to suggest ideas for new and exciting promotions. After all, it was at an employee brainstorming session that tapioca pearls first ended up in bubble tea in the first place all those years ago. Have a reward system in place for the employee who comes up with the promotion idea that generates the most sales.

Strategy #8: Set Up Booths at Sports Events

Based on your target market, it's a good idea to set up a booth or two at local school or college sports events. Advertise this extensively on your social media pages and around town. This is another simple way to interact with potential customers. It also increases your brand's presence in the community, which in turn works wonders for brand awareness.

Strategy #9: Create Specialized Google Ad Campaigns

Many small businesses are opting to use Google Ads to promote their businesses to a much wider audience. All you have to do is target key phrases related to bubble tea in your area and you will get your ads in front of potential customers. Furthermore, you can target specific demographics and locations, ensuring that your ad is only seen by people likely to be able to actually visit your store.

Strategy #10: Keep Abreast of Changing Trends

Keeping up-to-date with trends in the digital world is crucial to keeping your business relevant. Network with other boba shop owners, read blogs and online articles, and research new technologies and trends that will make your boba shop business processes simpler. Staying on top of current consumer trends in the bubble tea industry will let you know what your consumers are enjoying about the product and what changes they are looking for. It will also give your barista some fun new recipes and combinations to try out.

The Importance of Sharing Boba Tea Knowledge With Customers

It's essential to know that the more positive interaction you have with customers, the more likely they are to return to your business (and hopefully, bring friends). As you and your staff engage with customers, it's important to share your knowledge of bubble tea. Have conversations about the origins, types, and various flavors that you serve. You can also discuss the process. Doing this shows the consumer that you and your staff are passionate about your brand and know enough to be professionals in the industry. This, in turn, creates confidence in the product and the brand. When a consumer enjoys and feels comfortable with a brand, they will definitely become repeat customers!

Creating a Secondary Leg of Income

As you've been drawing up your business plan, factoring in costs, and assessing the amount of time, effort, and resources that need to go into creating a bubble tea shop, one question may have crossed your mind more than once: "Can you do all this by selling tea alone?" The good news is, you don't have to rely on your awesome boba drinks to single-handedly pay the rent, so to speak. Have you given any thought to using your boba brand to create a second leg of income?

I am, of course, referring to branded merchandise. It's not uncommon for big and small companies alike to rely on various types of merchandise to provide an additional income stream. This is also an excellent way to promote your brand because, once again, you have your brand name walking around town on a customer's t-shirt, backpack, or cap, and as I've mentioned before, it's advertising you didn't pay for! How do you go about creating brand merchandise income streams? It's simpler than you think!

1. Who Is Your Target Market?

Before you decide on the merchandise to create, you need to have a clear understanding of your store's particular target audience. That means, which demographic are you selling the most products to? Here, you want to be specific to your store. What happens in your store might not be a mirror image of the current industry trend. Spend some time analyzing the people who frequent your boba store the most. You can also review the analytics on your website. That will give you an idea of the demographic you should be creating merchandise for. This is important because some types of merchandise might be more appealing to your consumers.

2. Choose Products That Display Your Brand's Unique Vibe

The next step in choosing the perfect merchandise is based on your brand's unique vibe. When a customer looks at your merchandise, they need to instantly be able to associate it with your brand. For instance, if your brand identity is all about being environmentally friendly, then ideally, you'd opt for reusable backpacks that don't feature any plastic materials. Alternatively, if your vibe is more sporty, you'd opt for baseball caps and t-shirts with your logo on them. Here are a few of the more common merchandise ideas:

- clothing items such as t-shirts, hoodies, sweatshirts, and even long-sleeved shirts

- aluminum water bottles (people prefer these bottles to plastic, as it's more durable and also environmentally friendly—consider adding your logo to the front of the bottle)

- mugs (or even funky teacups, considering that you're a tea business!)

- backpacks for students, young and old, to use for schoolbooks or laptops

- tote bags to use for shopping to avoid having to use plastic

- notebooks or artbooks with your logo on the cover

- fridge magnets in the shape of a boba cup with your logo featured (that way, the customer will see your brand name every time they open the fridge!)

- caps, gloves, and scarves (great as a winter promotional offer)

- placemats or coasters

3. Create a Standard Design

You can opt to simply use your logo and your brand name, which would match your brand. Alternatively, you could create a different, but relatable image for your merchandise. Keep in mind that your customers—and other people who see the merchandise—should still be able to relate the design to your brand. If your brand logo is working for you, then it might be a good idea to just stick with the basics.

As you design your merchandise, it's a good idea to keep the following tips in mind:

- **Choose the right color:** Colors shouldn't clash with your logo colors. For instance, a yellow logo won't stand out on a yellow t-shirt. Opt for colors that highlight your logo. If your logo is light-colored, always opt for a dark background, and vice versa.

- **Opt for quality products:** A mistake some entrepreneurs make is that they opt for lower-quality merchandise to offset the cost. Keep in mind that if you're going to be selling the merchandise, it's never a good idea to push out inferior products. This will reflect badly on the brand and will defeat the whole purpose. To ensure that you don't get bogged down with the cost of merchandise, start small. You don't need 10 different merchandise options on day one. Customers will appreciate a quality item they can actually use rather than a t-shirt that shrinks after the first wash—or a backpack that has seams tearing on the second day. In the mind of a customer, the quality of your merchandise reflects the quality of your store products. If you're unsure of the type of merchandise to opt for, do an online poll on your social media pages, where you give your customers a few options to choose from.

- **Make and promote your merchandise:** When it comes to manufacturing your merchandise, consider partnering with a local supplier. You can promote their services on your website, again showing that your brand supports the local economy. Once your merchandise has been made, you need to promote it in the same way that you promote your boba products. Display a few items in-store and take professional photos for your website and different social media pages.

Tips on How to Use Your Boba Menu as a Marketing Tool

In addition to the usual (and the not-so-usual) marketing strategies you might implement to market your boba shop, there is another one you might not have given the attention it deserves. In short, have you thought of using your menu as a marketing tool? I'm sure you have a practical, yet stunning menu design in mind. You even know where on your counter you're going to place your stack of freshly printed menus. You may even have one enlarged or in a digital format above the counter, for customer convenience. Is that the extent of your menu planning? Few boba shop newbies realize that they can actually do so much more with their menus. Here are a few clever tips to help you turn your boba menu into a powerful marketing tool:

1. Create a Searchable Menu

Many times, potential consumers don't start an online search by typing in the name of the place they would like to order from, especially if they don't immediately know of a place that sells what they're looking for. That means your customer may start a search for boba drinks without ever having heard of your shop. For instance, they might search for "bubble tea drinks near me." This would be the most likely scenario for someone visiting the area or renting an Airbnb. To have your shop pop up in these searches, simply make your menu searchable by typing it out in HTML text. This simply means your menu is typed out directly on your website, rather than saved as an image. When you do this, your menu will easily be read by the Google crawlers that detect keywords based on search inputs. Any word on your menu that matches a consumer search will immediately make your menu available. It really doesn't get any easier than that!

2. Make Your Menu Mobile Friendly

Most internet users access the internet via their smart devices as opposed to logging into a PC or laptop. It's therefore essential to make your menu (and website) easily accessible and viewable on a mobile device. If your menu can be accessed at all times, from any type of device, then your customers will be able to engage with your brand at all times. In addition to that, both your menu and your website will rank higher in search engine algorithms, making it considerably easier for consumers to find you.

3. Keep It Relevant

Have you ever been to a place to order something you enjoy, only to be told it's no longer being served? Yet, there it is on the menu! Or perhaps you've been told that the promotion has ended, and the item is now back to the regular price? Annoying, right? And highly unprofessional! Make sure that you aren't doing the same to your customers. Menus should never be old or outdated—people will stop looking at them altogether. When you make any changes to your menu, make sure that the new version is updated to all the platforms and sites where your menu appears (even if it's a platform you don't often get much traffic from). If necessary, create a checklist for yourself or the person handling your social traffic and updates. List the places where you have placed the menu to avoid potentially forgetting to update one of your many platforms.

4. Put Your Menu Everywhere

I've mentioned this before: If a platform exists where you could potentially reach local customers, you need to upload your menu to it. This will ensure you reach the biggest audience possible. It also makes your boba shop very searchable. As your brand grows, you can root out the sites that don't really work for your type of business. Additionally, make it a rule that employees enquire from customers how they heard about the store. That will give you an idea of which platforms are working better than others. It's also an opportunity to increase marketing to the working platforms. Be sure to place your menu on travel sites that encourage local businesses to advertise, such as TripAdvisor.

5. Promote Your Menu Promotions Offer on Social Platforms

If you're planning particular specials for a limited time or as part of the holidays, it's crucial to update your social media pages. For these events, you can post a photo of the promo offer on your Facebook and Instagram pages every day for the duration of the promotion. Ensure that a clear date or time is highlighted to serve as a call to action. This will urge customers to act soon. This is also a super way to try out a new boba drink. Advertise that you have a new trial drink. Encourage customers to try it in-store and vote by liking the image of the drink on social media. If the drink reaches a certain number of likes by a certain date, it will be added to the menu.

6. Go Old-School

Another approach to consider is including an old-school approach to your menu distribution. Print quality copies of the latest menu and distribute them to all businesses around the area. That way, you will be reaching potential customers who are already close to the shop. While having an active online presence is crucial for any bubble tea business, it's important to not neglect some of the more traditional advertising approaches. Remember, the initial stages of your business are all about creating awareness for your product and location. And, while it may seem like the whole world is online, you'd be surprised to know how many people prefer to give it a miss. Still, following a few of the traditional (but affordable) advertising routes is a way to reach these people.

Key Takeaways

- Create a modern, engaging, and interactive website for your brand that highlights all the features of your products, brand, and general merchandise.
- Social media platforms are crucial to effective boba shop marketing.
- Sign up with Google Business, Yelp, TripAdvisor, and any other platform or website that encourages local business advertising.
- Get your boba shop involved with local community events to create brand awareness.
- Run frequent promotions and offer customers loyalty programs.
- Invest in specialized Google Ads.
- Stay updated with changing trends in the industry and on your social platforms.
- Consider adding branded merchandise as a secondary income stream.
- Your menu is a powerful marketing tool—get it on every platform possible.

Chapter 9:

Bubble Up: Franchising 101

When you're dreaming of setting up your own boba shop, one of the key questions to ask is, "To franchise or not?" One of the top reasons new business owners consider bubble tea franchise options has to do with the package deals on offer. Within these packages, boba entrepreneurs will find the right guidance and processes to follow to get their shops and brands up and running. An independent owner would have to figure these steps out by themselves as they go along. This is not only time-consuming but can affect business growth. With that said, let's take a look at a few top reasons why a boba franchise may be the best idea.

Reasons to Own a Bubble Tea Franchise

The franchise business model has numerous benefits which may just make it the perfect choice. Many boba entrepreneurs agree that following the franchise route simplifies the whole process, especially if you're stepping into business ownership for the first time.

Below, I've listed a few of the top reasons why opting for the franchise option is well worth considering.

1. You're Working With a Proven Business Model

With the sudden growth spurt in the bubble tea industry, prominent franchises are becoming more lucrative. This means that opting for a franchise gives you access to a proven business model that not only works, but is remarkably successful. Following an established business model will minimize mistakes and assist the boba entrepreneur to keep the process on track. A franchise business model helps you identify what needs to be done as well as the timeline that needs to be followed.

2. More Affordable Startup Costs

Depending on your current business finance budget, you might not think a boba franchise can be considered as having low or affordable startup costs. However, keep in mind that the average boba franchise costs between $50,000 and $150,000. This is considerably lower than the average food franchise. If you're working with a limited budget, a small franchise is a perfect option for you because you can always expand as your business evolves.

3. Potentially Higher Success Rates

It's a proven fact that franchise stores have a higher success rate than independents. For the most part, this has to do with consumers having more faith in what they believe to be an "established brand." This is partly because consumers know that franchises are regulated by certain health and quality regulations. In short, they know they will get a quality product at an affordable price.

4. Access to Certified Vendors

Picture this: As an independent boba shop owner, you will have to find the perfect vendors and suppliers. For the most part, this will involve a lot of trial and error. In some cases, this can be a very expensive learning curve. Ask yourself if you really have the time and resources to learn the hard way which suppliers are reliable. With a franchise, you get access to credited vendors and suppliers who are not only known within the industry but also know what each store needs and possibly how often stocks need to be replenished. These vendors will also be able to advise you of the products that other boba shops are using, and this could potentially give you the edge you need to not only become successful but *remain* successful.

5. Extensive Franchise Options to Choose From

With the demand for bubble tea growing at an exponential level all over the world, the market for franchises has also grown. That said, you'll have several different franchise options to choose from. You'll therefore be able to compare costs, packages, and branding options and easily find the franchise and business model that best suits your business goal.

How Exactly Do You Go About Getting a Boba Franchise?

If you've already made up your mind to opt for the franchise route, your next question will most likely be, "How do I find the perfect franchise opportunity?" It's important to compare options to your specific business goals. Essentially, you'll be asking yourself what each franchise package gives you versus what you need. Some simple steps to follow include those listed below.

Identify your target audience: Use the guidelines and tips discussed in Chapters 2 and 3 to decide who your target audience is. That's always your first step in setting up your own boba business.

Choose a concept: Next, you need to choose the concept that will give your specific target audience the desired experience. Essentially, there are three concepts to choose between: Firstly, there's grab-and-go, where consumers walk in, order, and leave. Secondly, you have dine-ins, where customers can sit in the store and possibly order food. A third option, commonly referred to as a hybrid option, refers to having a few tables and chairs on the sidewalk or outside on a balcony. Consumers collect their boba drinks (and possibly a food option) and sit down. There are usually only three or four tables in this concept. The concept you choose is a mixture between your boba goal and the location you can find.

Select a location: By using the guidelines outlined in Chapter 3, you'll be able to find the perfect location. Ensure that your proposed franchise requirements meet the necessary location needs.

Select a boba tea company: Once you know what type of general concept you want to go for, it'll be easier to choose the franchise that can help you reach that goal. Here, you need to decide if you want a store that's exclusively a bubble tea shop or if you want a tea and coffee shop that also serves food. Keep in mind that opting for stores that sell food will require additional licensing. There may also be additional compliance criteria from the health company.

Gather the funds: The amount of funds you need depends on the amount of cash you have as a down payment. You will then decide if you will loan the rest from a bank or lending company. Some franchises, such as Chatime and Bee & Tea, are on the affordable end of the boba franchise spectrum. Franchises such as Gong Cha and Jazen Tea lie on the higher end. Top franchises, such as Tapioca Express, can cost up to as much as $422,000. Kung Fung Tea, on the other hand, can set you back at least $250,000. It's important to keep in mind that there are additional costs that are made up of equipment, location funds, marketing, and even monthly royalty fees. Be sure to get a quote that highlights all these costs to avoid setbacks.

Get the necessary licenses: Boba franchises have specific requirements that potential boba entrepreneurs need to comply with before they can legally purchase the franchise. For the most part, these have to do with location, zoning licenses, location, duration of the contract, and store concept. These criteria are based on the Franchise Regulations set up for the US.

Set the system in place: Once you have complied with all the franchise requirements, the next step is to complete the necessary training. You'll then start ordering your ingredients and setting up your store and website branding.

Potential Boba Franchises to Consider

Part of what makes the bubble tea shop concept so appealing is the many franchise options on offer. With a wide variety of cost packages, it's easy to find an option that fits just about every budget. To make finding the perfect boba franchise considerably easier, I've compiled a list of some of the more popular choices. The costs listed are at the end of 2022.

Franchise Name	Estimated Initial Cost (Excluding product and royalty fee costs)	Founded In	Franchise Type
Tapioca Express	$130,000 +	2000	Largest bubble tea franchise in the US

Chatime	$160,000	2005	Bubble tea franchise started in Taiwan
Jazen Tea	$186,000 - $340,000	2013	Tea cafe specializing in fruit and bubble teas smoothies slushies
HTeaO	$289,000 - $859,000	2018	Bubble tea specialty shop with a very extensive boba tea menu
Bee & Tea	$150,000	2014	Bubble tea shops specializing in boba drinks made with honey
Ninja Bubble Tea	Available on request	2013	Bubble tea shop that also sells: organic

			coffee smoothies convenience foods
Sweet Rolled Tacos	$160,000 +	2016	Convenience cafe that specializes in bubble tea
Glow Tea	$200,000 +	2o21	Specializes in high-quality boba tea
Gong Cha	$178,000 - $335,000	2006 (originally from Taiwan)	Specialized bubble tea using original Taiwanese recipes and methods
AraVita	$114,000 - $180,000	2016	Specializes in: coffee smoothies specialty bubble tea
Sweetwaters Coffee &	$260,000 - $390,000	2004	Specialty coffee

Tea			bubble tea stores
Sharetea	$100,000 - $300,000	1992	bubble tea brewed iced teas signature mocktails ice-blended coffees
DRNK Coffee + Tea and QWENCH Juice Bar	$253,000 - $693,000	2015	coffee bubble tea smoothies food
Bubble-ology	$205,850	2011	bubble tea bubble waffles snacks

Franchise Costs

A simple Google search of potential franchise costs can be confusing. That's because many articles focus on total start-up costs while others mention initial investor buy-in. Before you base your preliminary budget on a cost you've researched, it's essential to know what the cost is usually made up of. Fortunately, the FTC Franchise Rule stipulates that franchisors must provide potential franchisees (you, the boba shop owner) with an itemized account of the *entire* estimated initial investment. This includes factors such as opening inventory, initial training, signage, rent, and security deposit, to name a few.

Additionally, there are four terms that you must familiarize yourself with when you start researching franchise options. These are:

- **Initial investment:** An initial investment can best be described as a deposit paid for you to start the franchise ownership process. In some instances, it's just a broader scope of the franchise fee.
- **Total investment:** As the name implies, a total investment refers to the total amount of the investment. This makes it the bottom amount, so to speak.
- **Franchise Fee:** Your franchise fee covers the cost of your application, initial marketing, advertising, training, and general costs to get your store set up as well as the sales commission to the franchisor. In the event of cancellation, the franchise fee is non-refundable. So, don't pay any fees or sign any documents until you are 100 percent comfortable with the choice you've made.
- **Royalty fees:** These are the fees that the franchisor collects from your business every month. These fees are also calculated as a certain percentage of your monthly revenue. Currently, there's no set standard for the

percentage. For the most part, you can expect to pay between four and 12 percent, depending on the franchise packages.

Consider Kiosk Options

If you're a little taken aback by the actual costs of bubble tea franchises, you'll be happy to know that the Bubbleology franchise has a potential solution for you. They are one of the few franchises that give you the option to host a kiosk within a local market or shopping mall, as opposed to an actual more conventional brick-and-mortar storefront. Choosing this option will be considerably cheaper and works well for entrepreneurs who want to gain working knowledge in the industry while they save up for a franchise store package.

Key Takeaways

- There are several benefits to opting for a franchise other than choosing to do it independently—professional guidance and access to certified vendors are among the top advantages.
- With the wide variety of boba franchises to choose from, you will easily find one that matches your business goal and your budget.

- There is a considerable amount of costs that may not be mentioned in the initial bubble tea franchise quote, so be sure to request a concise quote before you approach your lender.

Chapter 10:

Bubble Tea Recipe Ideas

Finally, the fun part of running a boba shop: creating delicious bubble tea. While boba started out as just a few traditional recipes, the concept has evolved so much over the years that there are now an incredible number of options to choose from. That said, how do you know what recipes to put on your menu? The good news is that your menu isn't written in stone and you can amend, tweak, and adjust it as your business grows. Many boba entrepreneurs start with a combination of the classics and include a few designer variations as they start getting to know their customer base. Before I share some firm favorites to try, let me share a few tips to help you choose the best boba recipes for your shop.

Tips to Choose the Best Boba Recipes

Bubble tea is the reason your store is open, and it should always be your top priority. Consider a few of these tips when you're shortlisting options for your menu:

- When you do your initial market research, be sure to ask potential customers what flavors they currently enjoy and which they would be interested in trying.

- Be willing to tweak your menu after finding that some variations don't do well, as this will enable you to cater to a wider audience.
- Add different design options that will enable you to cater to a wider audience.
- Spend time in other bubble tea stores or check out their online options to see what flavors your competitors are offering.
- Choose recipes that fit your business model but don't stray too far from what makes bubble tea so unique.
- Look for interesting ways to present your boba to customers.
- Create a suggestion box in-store, as well as an online equivalent where customers or visitors can suggest new flavors to try out. Arrange a prize for the flavor recommendation that gains the most interest (the prize can be branded merchandise or a few in-store vouchers).
- Include a wide variety of topping choices on your menu to make customization simple and unique—make note of the most popular creations and consider adding a few to your menu.
- Have in-store "flavor of the week" promotions where you include test flavors and customers can go online and vote for their preferred new variations.

- Include healthy alternatives that are made with green tea, soy milk, and low sugar.
- Offer milkshakes and smoothies made to blend in with the bubble tea theme.

Fun Bubble Tea Recipes to Try

Drawing up your first menu can be daunting. If you're going to be employing a boba barista, that might make the process considerably easier, as they can assist by making popular suggestions. If you're starting out solo, the good news is that there are a few of the more common boba recipe options on my website to get you started. As a bonus, I want to include a few of them here. I also want to add a few that I've recently discovered.

1. Traditional Bubble Tea

A classic bubble tea drink is a must on every boba menu. Despite the hundreds of flavor choices, there are loyal boba drinkers who prefer the classics. And, since few things beat an original classic, be sure to include it. However, it has to be said that there are as many versions of the classics as there are new variations!

Ingredients

- 1 cup tapioca pearls
- 4 cups freshly brewed black tea (a strong brew is always recommended)
- 1 tablespoon sugar
- ½ cup whole milk (any milk of your choice—almond, soy, or even oat are popular alternatives to dairy)
- Ice cubes

Directions

1. Add sugar to the hot/warm tea and stir thoroughly
2. Allow to cool and refrigerate until chilled—no more than two hours before serving
3. Place tapioca in the cups
4. Put the milk, ice, and tea in a shaker
5. Strain the tea mixture into your cup
6. Serve with a wide straw

2. Strawberry Matcha Latte

No bubble tea menu is complete without at least one strawberry-flavored boba on it—and the Strawberry Matcha Latte is just the one to consider.

Ingredients

- 2 teaspoons of matcha
- 2 ¼ cups of filtered water
- **⅓ cup of strawberry syrup**
- ¼ cup of tapioca pearls
- ¾ cup of milk
- ¾ cup of ice (preferably made from filtered water)

Directions

1. Cook tapioca balls as usual
2. Make matcha by combining ¼ cup water and matcha in your shaker—ensure that it's well shaken.
3. Assemble the boba by placing warm tapioca into the bottom of the cup and add the strawberry syrup. Add the ice, milk, and matcha by pouring the drink directly onto the layers to keep the layers separated.
4. Serve immediately and stir before drinking. Use a wide straw to suck up the tapioca balls.

3. Peanut Bubble Tea

Who wouldn't love a cup of fresh peanut bubble tea? (With this one, be sure to advise customers of the peanut content in case of allergies, of course.)

Ingredients

- ½ cup of tapioca pearls
- ¼ cup fresh peanut butter
- 3 tbsp honey
- 1 cup light soy beverage (no sugar added)
- 1 cup brewed black tea, cooled
- 1 cup ice cubes

Directions

1. Cook the tapioca as usual
2. Rinse with cold water to cool
3. Whisk peanut butter and honey until blended
4. Gradually stir in the milk
5. Add the tea of your choice
6. Spoon tapioca into the serving glass
7. Add the tea mixture to the ice and serve with a wide straw

4. Oolong Bubble Tea

Oolong bubble tea is very popular in Taiwan, and I have it often when I'm there. For the most part, oolong is a tea that has been processed halfway between green and black tea. You might have to order it online or from a specialized tea shop, but it will be well worth the effort. Always opt for the roasted Taiwanese varieties. Also, the sachets or bags create considerably less mess!

Ingredients

- 1 ¾ cup of filtered water
- 2 sachets (or tea bags) of oolong tea
- 3 tbsp dark brown sugar (for added sweetness)
- ¼ cup of milk
- ¾ cup of ice
- 2 shots of espresso
- ¼ cup of tapioca pearls

Directions

1. Make the tea by steeping the oolong tea in hot water for 5 minutes and cool
2. Discard tea sachets and stir in brown sugar
3. Set aside to cool
4. Cook tapioca pearls as usual
5. Assemble the drink by adding warm tapioca balls in brown sugar syrup into a glass
6. Add ice, cooled tea, and milk

7. Serve immediately and stir before serving. Use a wide straw to enjoy the tapioca

5. Oreo Bubble Milk Tea

Oreo cookies are one of those ingredients that people add to just about anything to enhance the flavor. Bubble tea is no exception!

Ingredients

- ½ cup tapioca pearls
- ¼ cup brown sugar
- 2 tbsp water
- 1 cup milk (any type will do, although oat milk is a favorite)
- 5–6 Oreo cookies with cream removed (add a few for serving)
- 1–2 scoops vanilla or coconut ice cream
- Whipped cream (regular or coconut flavored)
- Crushed ice cubes

Directions

1. Prepare the tapioca pearls as usual
2. Make a brown sugar syrup and add the strained tapioca

3. Blend the Oreos, ice cream, and tea until smooth
4. Spoon 2–3 tbsp of tapioca into the cup
5. Top the tapioca with a handful of ice
6. Pour the Oreo milk over the tapioca and ice
7. Top with whipped cream and crushed Oreos
8. Serve with a large straw for the tapioca pearls

6. Taro Bubble Tea

Taro bubble tea is made from the powder of a starchy root very similar to a potato. While originally cultivated in Asia, it's now enjoyed around the world as a food and a bubble tea. A fun feature of this drink is that the taro powder gives the boba a purple color, making it both tasty and colorful!

Ingredients

- Green or black tea
- Tapioca pearls
- 1 tbsp milk
- 1 tbsp sweetener (simple syrup is an easy choice to use)
- 1 ½ tbsp taro root powder
- ¾ cup of ice

Directions

1. Prepare tapioca pearls as usual
2. Brew the tea as required
3. Blend the brewed tea, sweetener (or syrup), taro powder, and ice until smooth
4. Add tapioca pearls to the cup
5. Pour the drink over the cooled tapioca
6. Serve with a wide straw

7. Iced Latte With Boba

It was only a matter of time before the coffee lovers of the world found a way to enjoy the tapioca pearls that make bubble tea so famous! If you want to give any potential coffee-loving customers a reason to stop by your store, this recipe is definitely it. It's worth mentioning that this particular boba isn't served as cold as some of the other recipes. With its coffee element, the tapioca is served warm, and not hot, as you don't want anyone scalding their mouth!

Ingredients

- ¾ cups of filtered water
- 2 tbsp of brown sugar
- 2 shots espresso
- ¼ cup of tapioca pearls
- 1 cup of ice
- ¾ cup of milk (any kind)

Directions

1. Cook tapioca pearls as usual and mix them with sugar syrup
2. Pour cooked tapioca and syrup into a cup
3. Add ice, as tapioca should be warm, not hot
4. Pour the milk directly on the ice to keep the layers separated
5. Add the espresso by pouring it directly onto the ice rather than into the mix—this is important to keep the layers separated
6. This boba doesn't get any additional toppings, in keeping with the look of a coffee drink

8. Bubble Tea Ice Cream

One of the ways to keep your menu engaging is to add other products that have a bubble tea flair. And what better way to do that than with a boba ice cream?

Ingredients

- 500 ml black tea (Assam is a good choice here, although any will do)
- 5 g sugar
- 2 scoops vanilla ice cream
- Ice

Directions

1. Fill a 500 ml shaker cup with ice
2. Add 500 ml black tea
3. Use your fructose dispenser to add 5–10 g of sugar
4. Place this mixture in your shaker machine for about eight seconds
5. Pour the mixture into a 700 ml boba glass
6. Add two scoops of vanilla ice cream
7. Seal and serve

9. Peppermint Moringa Bubble Tea

Peppermint is one of those flavors that you add to an assortment of drinks and foods to provide a crisp, fresh flavor profile. And the refreshing sweetness of peppermint doesn't disappoint in its boba version.

Ingredients

- 2 bags of moringa tea with peppermint (or any other tea with a robust peppermint flavor)
- tapioca pearls
- 1–2 cups of milk (almond works particularly well in this recipe)
- A handful of ice cubes
- Fresh mint for garnish

Method

1. Prepare tapioca as usual
2. Brew tea and place it in the fridge to cool
3. Pour tapioca into your cup
4. Place a few ice cubes on top of the tapioca
5. Pour the brewed mint tea over the ice cubes
6. Top off with milk, garnish leaves, and add a wide straw

10. Fresh Mango Bubble Tea Smoothie

As with the boba ice cream, adding a few bubble tea-type smoothies to the menu will only add to your variety and potentially increase sales. One of my favorite boba smoothies is the mango bubble tea smoothie. Not only is it super tasty, but its bright color adds flair to all those awesome social media promotional photos you're going to be taking. Additionally, many boba shop owners have a section dedicated primarily to smoothies. With the wide variety of fruits and fruit syrups available, the opportunities are endless!

Ingredients

- 100 ml of blended mango or mango syrup (fresh fruit is always better, as it enhances the freshness of your smoothie)
- 2 scoops of bubble tea coconut powder
- 1 cup of ice

- 2 scoops of cooked tapioca pearls
- Several pieces of fresh mango

Directions

1. Blend all the ingredients except the tapioca
2. Pour tapioca pearls in a cup
3. Pour the blended mix over the tapioca pearls in your cup
4. Add fresh pieces of mango on top
5. Seal the cup and serve with a wide straw

Additional Tips for Preparing Boba Drinks

If you're going to hire a professional boba barista, you might not need this next section. However, as a business owner, you must know exactly how everything in your business works, and that includes how to make the best version of each boba drink on your menu. If you're not employing a boba barista right off the bat, it means you're going to have to perfect the art of making bubble tea before you open your doors.

While boba-making is essentially making tea with extras, the reality is, you can make a bad boba. And that will be the quickest way to turn customers away. To avoid that, I'd like to share a few boba-making tips that are crucial to know, whether you're making simple bubble tea recipes or more complex designer variations.

- **Water:** Wherever possible, use filtered water to make the tea and ice. Not only is filtered water healthier, but it's also less harmful to your tea-making machines. Filtered water also doesn't have chemical undertones, making your drink tastier.

- **Cooking tapioca:** Your tapioca pearls should always be cooked at the time you're going to make the drink. Tapioca can't be made ahead of time, as it starts hardening after about three hours, making it difficult to chew and rather unpleasant. The golden rule of boba preparation is that the tapioca pearls *always* go into the cup or glass first.

- **Brewing the tea:** Unlike tapioca, tea can be made in advance. You can keep it in the fridge for up to four days. Doing that means it will already be cool when you need to make your boba drink. Furthermore, you don't have to use the best tea on the market, which means tea bags or tea sachets will work just fine. Plus, there won't be the mess that working with loose tea creates. Regular black or green tea are excellent options that work well with bubble tea drinks.

- **Milk:** The good news is that any milk can be used. This means you can offer soy or plant-based alternatives such as almond to customers who don't drink dairy. Options like whole milk or half and half always make a drink creamier, which is a handy tip to know if you want a super creamy drink! Be sure to make a note of milk choices on your menu so that people who don't drink dairy know you can cater to them.

- **Sugar:** Essentially, brown sugar goes better with cooking tapioca, especially if you're going to be using a robust tea such as oolong. Many boba baristas prefer brown sugar in all boba drinks, but you can easily use white granulated sugar.
- **Fruit syrup:** It's also a good idea to stock up on a variety of fruit syrups for those customized drink orders or even special smoothie requests. In addition to flavor, syrups add color to your boba.
- **Fresh fruit:** Adding fresh fruits to your bubble tea or smoothies offers your customers a delicious and healthy treat. And since fruit is naturally sweet, it reduces the need for additional sugar. Once again, having fresh fruit on hand shows health-conscious customers that you've included them in your menu.
- **Layering your ingredients:** The appeal of some boba drinks lies in the layered looks of different colors and flavors. Simply pouring your ingredients into the glass won't create the layered look you're trying to create. The secret to effective layering is as follows:

Add the sweetest ingredients to the bottom of the cup. Then, work your way up with the less sweet ingredients. Always pour the ingredients onto the ice very slowly so that the layers develop as you're creating the drink.

Key Takeaways

- There are thousands of ways to make boba drinks—your menu will never be short of fun and tasty combinations.
- Include a variety of flavors that when displayed together create a colorful and appealing image (remember your marketing).
- It isn't necessary to use the most expensive loose teas—tea bags or sachets will work just fine!
- Any milk will do, which includes options such as soy, almond, oat, and even coconut.
- Always make tapioca fresh and never more than two hours before you need it.
- Check out my website for more boba-preparing tips to get you started!

And Finally...

I've mentioned this before: In my daily dealings with bubble tea enthusiasts, the number one question I'm asked is, "Where does a person even begin when they're considering a boba business?" That was my inspiration to compile the most significant guidelines to get you started on your boba journey. Let's recap the steps you need to follow:

1. Familiarize yourself with the *entire* boba concept—be sure it's what you want to do to avoid wasting time and resources.

2. Review the pros and cons of all scenarios and find potential solutions to the cons before you start making plans.

3. Calculate the costs and expenses required to establish the capital needed, and research potential business loans or investment offers.

4. Find the perfect location by doing extensive research as well as site and market surveys. Ensure you ask the right questions.

5. Create an initial business plan with as much detail as possible, covering all aspects of your growing business. Research the sales figures, costs, and strategies of top bubble tea franchises to see how you can incorporate them into your own plan.

6. Approach lenders or investors to secure the necessary capital. Save as much money as possible so that you have to borrow less—check out small business loan offers in your area.

7. Compare the pros and cons of running an independent business versus a franchise (keep in mind that franchises come with lucrative packages that provide access to perks such as supplier, training, and signage).

8. Invest in quality machines, supplies, and ingredients—where possible, opt for vendors who can supply you with all (or the majority of) the products you'll need to avoid the stress of dealing with multiple vendors.

9. Create a website and update your social media business profiles—remember to include business listings such as Yelp and Google Business.

10. Give marketing and branding the attention it deserves—think outside of the box, and when in doubt, try everything!

11. Hire and train employees—place extensive focus on getting the right manager and boba barista, as they will make all the difference to your store's eventual success.

12. Create a few different menu design options to see which works best on all of your social platforms—make your menu searchable and compatible with all devices.

13. Test your recipes to ensure they are tastier and better presented than those served by your competitors—adjust where necessary and keep your menu relevant.
14. Set up your store and create hype on all your platforms, as well as in the community.
15. Arrange a massive grand opening sale—be sure to advertise on all your socials and post photos daily.

Setting up your own bubble tea shop can be a lot of fun. Furthermore, with the right planning, the process will be easier than you might have anticipated. Use the guides and tips I've provided to get each phase of the planning process started. Keep in mind that the average bubble tea shop usually serves between 100–300 bubble tea drinks each day. Stores that have the added advantage of an excellent location can easily sell between 500–1000, plus boba drinks on a busy day. Sounds pretty lucrative, right?

Finally, I'd like to say that although many people regard bubble tea as the fad of the moment, it's worth reminding you that it's been growing in strength for two decades with no signs of slowing down. Although this delicious bubble drink started at a humble tea stand, it's now sold in bubble tea stores, coffee shops, and restaurants around the world. There's no reason why you shouldn't be a part of the hype!

Take that first step to becoming a bubble tea shop owner and be sure to check out my website for the supplies you need to get started. Happy selling!

References

BubbleTeaology. (2022, June 30). *Why is a commercial bubble tea machine important?* BubbleTeaology. https://www.bubble tea ology.com/why-is-a-commercial-bubble-tea-machine-important/

Buenaventura, A. (2020, August 4). *Booky guide.* https://booky.ph/blog/milk-tea-recipes/

Chatter, F. (2022, October 16). *The best tea franchises of 2022.* Franchise Chatter. https://www.franchisechatter.com/2022/10/15/the-best-tea-franchises-of-2022/

Chon, W. (2020, July 31). *Garden Grove, California is the boba capital of the US.* Medium. https://towardsdatascience.com/garden-grove-california-is-the-boba-capital-of-the-us-1f98c1293ae7

Corner, A. (2019, April 9). *10 Logo design tips to take your brand to the next level [+ Logo Templates].* Venngage. https://venngage.com/blog/logo-design-tips/

Emily. (2022, July 17). *Oreo bubble milk tea (Cookies and Cream Boba).* Thank You Berry Much. https://tyberrymuch.com/oreo-bubble-milk-tea-boba/#mv-creation-192-jtr

Erway, C. (2017, June 29). *Classic Bubble Tea Recipe*.
Epicurious.
https://www.epicurious.com/recipes/food/vie
ws/classic-bubble-tea-recipe

Espina, D. (2019, January 21). *Paper Bubble Tea Products*.
BubbleTeaology.   https://www.bubble
teaology.com/paper-bubble-tea-
products/#:~:text=These%20paper%20cups%
20are%20a

fastfwd. (2021, September 6). *Why is brandingiImportant?*
10 key reasons why it matters. Fastfwd.
https://www.fastfwd.com/why-branding-is-
important/

Future Market Insights, F. M. (2022, September 1).
Bubble   tea   market.   FMI.
https://www.futuremarketinsights.com/reports
/bubble-tea-
market#:~:text=The%20current%20valuation
%20of%20the,billion%20by%20the%20year%2
02032.

Hanson, G. (2022, May 23). *5 reasons to own A bubble tea*
franchise.   TEAlicious   Franchising.
https://tealiciousfranchising.com/bubble-tea-
franchise/

Jardinel, D. (2019, May 29). *A café owner's guide to*
scheduling.   Perfect   Daily   Grind.
https://perfectdailygrind.com/2019/05/a-cafe-
owners-guide-to-scheduling/

MacDonnell, K. (2022, June 10). *Delicious taro milk tea recipe (Easy Steps!)*. Coffee Affection. https://coffeeaffection.com/taro-milk-tea-recipe/

Martins, A. T. (2019, August 23). *Best bubble tea shop franchise in 2022 [Top 10 Picks]*. MomAndPopFranchise. https://www.momandpopfranchise.com/bubble-tea-opportunities/

Medved, K. (2021, August 11). *Tips for hiring, training & keeping your cafe employees happy*. Bites. https://mybites.io/blog/tips-for-hiring-training-keeping-your-cafe-employees-happy/

Melore, C. (2022, March 18). *Tea, coffee, or water? Here's what your go-to daily drink says about you*. Study Finds. https://studyfinds.org/millennials-coffee-tea-water/

Mike, M. (2019, February 20). *How to open a bubble tea shop*. BubbleTeaology. https://www.bubbleteaology.com/how-to-open-a-bubble-tea-shop/

Navarro, L. (2021, November 7). *Tips for successful coffee shop management*. Texas Coffee School. https://texascoffeeschool.com/tips-for-successful-coffee-shop-management/

Mike, M. (2022a, July 22). *Strawberry matcha latte bubble tea*. BubbleTeaology. https://www.bubbleteaology.com/strawberry-matcha-latte-bubble-tea/

Mike, M. (2022b, August 1). *Oolong bubble tea (Oolong boba milk Tea)*. BubbleTeaology. https://www.bubbleteaology.com/oolong-bubble-tea-oolong-boba-milk-tea/

Palo Alto Software. (2016, January 30). *Tim Berry*. Planning, startups, stories. https://timberry.bplans.com/10-benefits-of-business-planning-for-all-businesses/

Soocial. (n.d.). *Soocial.com*. Soocial.com; Soocial.com. https://www.soocial.com/bubble-tea-statistics/

Squires, E. (2016b, March 9). *5 tips for hiring the perfect barista*. Perfect Daily Grind. https://perfectdailygrind.com/2016/03/5-tips-for-hiring-the-perfect-barista/

Statistica. (2022, November 28). *Statistica*. Statistica. https://www.statista.com/statistics/266465/number-of-starbucks-stores-worldwide/#:~:text=Total%20Starbucks%20locations%20globally%202003%2D2022&text=There%20were%2035%2C711%20thousand%20Starbucks%20stores%20worldwide%20in%202022.

team. (2018, July 3). *What makes a good logo: The dos and don'ts of logo design*. NoCodeBA. https://www.wix.com/blog/2018/07/good-logo-design-tips/

Turner, M. L. (2017, February 28). *Is now the right time to franchise your business Concept?* Forbes. https://www.forbes.com/sites/marciaturner/2

017/02/28/is-now-the-right-time-to-franchise-your-business-concept/?sh=2557d9e91439